TALE LIGHT

£12-

TALE LIGHT

NEW & SELECTED POEMS 1984–2009

Karen Mac Cormack

BookThug | West House Books

Cover Image of Nanoparticle Formation by Patrick Coleman Saunders, Victoria Interrante, and Sean C. Garrick, University of Minnesota.

Co-published by BookThug and West House Books

BookThug: 53 Ardagh Street, Toronto, Ontario M6S 1Y4, Canada
www.bookthug.com

West House Books: 40 Crescent Road, Sheffield S7 1HN, United Kingdom
www.westhousebooks.co.uk

The production of this book was made possible through the generous assistance of the Canada Council for the Arts and the Ontario Arts Council.

LIBRARY AND ARCHIVES CANADA CATALOGUING IN PUBLICATION

Mac Cormack, Karen, 1956–
　　　Tale light: new & selected poems, 1984–2009 / Karen Mac Cormack.

ISBN CA 978-1-897388-54-9 | ISBN UK 978-1-904052-26-5

I. Title.

PS8575.C67T35 2010　　　C811'.54　　　C2010-901839-7

TABLE OF CONTENTS

... to see any given object as an assemblage of aspects,
rather than as something bound by space and time.

— J.M. COHEN

for my Cushla

PREFACE

My decision not to include collaborative work (previously published in book form) proved to be a difficult one, though it still seems appropriate on the eve of TALE LIGHT's publication. This accounts for the absence of poems from *Fit To Print* (with Alan Halsey), and *From A Middle* (with Steve McCaffery). *Multiplex* (with Ron Silliman) was never a collaboration. (On the occasion of a mini-reading tour together in California in 1998 our respective poems were published in a chap book by Wild Honey Press.) Nor is there any excerpt from *Implexures* (Complete Edition, 2008), as it is polybiography, albeit one in which poetic forces impact throughout. I have revised and amended certain poems reprinted herein (especially with the intent that typographical errors be corrected). Prefatory material from earlier titles appears at the end of this new and selected, or selected and new, which signals to the author that implexifying is her chosen way of writing, indeed.

KAREN MAC CORMACK
February 2010

from NOTHING BY MOUTH (1984)

•

in the editing of a current violence
the planes are increasingly
full

villages white

blisters in the night eclipse
mouth upturned and open
where the eye is not a vowel

in a hierarchy of information
left and right are both
west of the period. This is

not a vertical introduction or insertion
of content these miles imply removal from
the quiet,

interrupted uneven
horizontal fingers of other islands
an intermittent line irrigated
green one can glimpse through
the continuation of sky moving south
to the ground each successive stone to

a house by the sea
shutters on windows
moonlight slatted coolly
on a marble floor

where a blindness due to rooves
listens not to cats but those
cries in the courtyard nightly

all this romance because an artery functions
inarticulate
in a uniform blackout palms of the hands in
a fan's spreading
to describe the scene
cooling what is vaporous knotted
once pulled
taut in a line
the boys practice arrogance all day

capsizing bottles Solution or capital
letters
in the darkroom end of to end
air breathing in   tincture

un uomo chi fa la pietra

for I.L.

i

a man stands in a circle of exclamation
marks

he arranges stones to resemble

glyphs

granite

aloud he reads
quartz and travertine he raises:
question marks

ii

water flows over but electricity does not
require cooling.   the separation

bleeds white in a river.   pebbles
recirculate.

iii

columns are turned
surfaces he is conversant with

striation
in so many pauses, a clustered
phrase

ground under angles
acid makes legible

iv

a mortarless document
optic bridge

his (preference
is seldom)
to punctuate

for Stella

if two people standing on the same line
ten miles apart face each other
will they perceive a common mirage(?)

consider her aerially.
there is evidence. it does not adjust
to air currents or degrees of

a circle formed along latitudes and longitudes
and equal points in between: will its
centre be the focus of collective attention(?)

the time wind takes to meet the resistance of
what protects bone. shattered
fragile pearls there are. no clues

for those at right angles to one another
how many mutual facts will they perceive
at the point of intersection(?)

●

there is a blue where what we form together
lives

the edges of this taste of nebulae, a pulse
accrete(d) beating

to sense exchange entering
female and male

it is
rapport

it does not rely on exits through
these open doors

distilled indigo
in(d)i go

from STRAW CUPID (1987)

"loco citato"

harness the telling a spur-line "the bit described"
in the middle of horticultural   prominent passed

locus

wouldn't be any other sound to the here a chemical once did that
on either side of its story
once Upon the train the stillness ceased to employ so many spaces
colours torched
without parallel friction the points of gesture

its news is current
water has no bones
shape of a sight how far the distance carries itself
at a time

the hour arrived from
constraint to keep light in the house
sections of sky but not blue in the glass not a mirror stopping not
a cork flotation yes

set a retina
a saucer leaves the future sipped away
this delicacy of part between the eyes and the spine
let us green

the coil of hip so walking out
principle of knot moveable
or the stubbornness of a whittled topic
how kept a body from self-separation
that angle again and the leather wears from heel to toe
I do not consider pilgrims in

words

no, the train has stopped a related station not the same
of a situation more than a body
inhabits limbo   hem lowered
                 to the ground by night flares
                 the music of border information

exercise intimidates
and recalls a transport the wheels drew nearer to in themselves
away from an opacity linked to the not-known

not what is forgotten

in a story
this quality of light does not necessarily elucidate
something else in a vehicle
or outside it

a cat sits under its coat and you went looking for blankets
night light
thread and bare feet drum siren
see the ticket is still valid

meridian obliqued every quarter
which part of the hand multiplied texture of paper
a magician would sue
or put it down to a moot audience on the Local

carrier/haberdasher
the window seat and who reads the Times
he was or she knew better since oratory
the mouth a month takes in if pleasure would halve it
each might be assort to strew and not so early in an even

time never leaves itself alone
in the dark   night rents   a room

crustacean so design told its corners to relax and have another pillow
tale on another movement

superimposed velocities and that handerkerchief
if a certainty debunked the mention

on all fours a sphere rested   orb to wear
item on a list and a planet retinue

switching (for H.B.)

a)

reassembling voice from ceiling to floor
from cell to synapse what the eye doesn't see
will hurt
between the two not a reference, this is the switch
known black along handle
fingers on the detector the false security
check the hand moving to the pocket
Demanding a sum of self: subsiding
in appropriation a tense given taken

b)

flesh relates to air, conditioned through the heart sinking
what is the body to temperature: site mobile
steel a shape of cooled heat the rehearsal
of separation
the word KILL is one way streets have
to do with this broken line
too-dimensional a number of intensities
in the fray knocking

A Singular Plurality

Sometimes the words arise from the outside and lips form around them, providing a receptacle where they lodge as sounds repeated for many (y)ears.

They spread from small unit to larger until a majority is declared in effect.

Considered dangerous, each group is jealous of the other(s).

One word enjoys equal prominence with every persuasion. It comes to mean more than all the other words formerly employed when each unit was/is small.

Leaders are those members who gain control of any given group. Most members aspire to leadership and because this is not possible, struggles commence. The member(s) who best manipulate(s) words the other members choose to hear, become(s) their leader(s).

The leader(s) often find(s) it necessary to share (the word) power in a number of ways, i.e. pretending to acknowledge the validity of words expressed by members of other groups.

The same words are employed by all. It is the inflection or position of any given word that contributes to the meaning the individual or unit intends to convey.

Often these words are amplified by technological means, as well as appearing on surfaces such as paper.

things   (Tahitian)

dustbins will never be the same duty to again concern what the eye sees
to believe
they always used to fall to their knees and now they just beg
on a certain page in that novel the curve is radiant
and usually, or don't browsers notice these things in the racks
better dressed, arero mona[†], everyone is more expensive

there is no such thing as triumph, only more
He loved her.
what did that have to do with the rest of his life?

every last thing has a beginning
taking the change to heart the book never left in his (sweet tongue[†])
the pocket

Love is not a Location

to ride side-saddle: casual
                        causal

        the result of a fall

calumny   columns apart

stealth of tracking to the power of one

how many footprints   inhabit the earth
and who is the desert   precursor of glass
                        each breath's tiny shape
to fuse a hair
construe a demeanour
move swiftly that notion, or miss

a reign impaired this mention only
sunday in the turnpike words the ear brailles

any way the world begins spinning
is a departure
at x number of feet and falling in centimetres
is to understand more than one lingo in jungle parameter
        l
        o
        n
        g
        i
and l a t i t u d e of a string
        u   composes knot
        d
        e

only hours in Wadi Halfa

failure to a pulled string would not be an instrument
tuned to any perfection other than .

the outward reach
does   knowledge   equal Africa
        will   ever

leave electricity out of this cube and look at the sky
accumulated shadow rising
if bones are measure to flesh
these fires fly

in the north of intention
final word of every sentence and
the question mark upside down with exclamation

cold muscles are taut to demand a graduated
longing for lengthening heat

hands seek not to meet but round a change in temperature
vertical keening the white voice hums beneath its separate selves

not conversant with the audial
simmering of individual colours in a lake
there are animals too and radar to track them
newspapers get left behind with the crumbs, on what is
remembered as a table

never to have lived in the place of birth
denotes a photographic memory
black and white, a false order in the garden's
banana sprawl and papaya abundance,
mangoes: two men leaving and the snake the dog caught

they are   everywhere   tongues prove
          but no vipers in Eire   without voice

möbius knotted a singular passion for retrieval

the miles discuss among themselves the many feet to Mecca
a continent's accounting
of mouths and tea, kilometres commodity
green reckoning on rains a season temporary
bending heads to an horizon astonished
by itself reluctantly

south of
the equator might foresee itself backwards
and no one believes in the need for harpsichords
when Victoria falls
that height and the lady agree

Clementine and a ½

Part I

"We are all mortal too early." – D.W. Griffith

"The bible's written in a way you'd better not take too literally."
— I. Lazarus

a miracle rode in the ear on a rainy day and
relocates speech   an hour so bruised
headway making that
                carry another twenty-three and one has a new date
constant of concept

a freeway produces exotica and heart chimes cochineal, lemons two-
dimensional setting "yellow" plus "shape"

we are at the off-set-out on a hotel bed with aptitude in mind
five-fingered roundabout spleen and transom

square root of rain is
                "fall"

Salt grown women's heads level-tabled.
A man in a boat comes fixative vituperative.
Lengths breadth rose.

an eye absorbs
    coals reflect

rented November
room, smoke or marble-handled heat
sizes

the query makes its entrance source
and outcome held on either side and the miracle
choosing neither caresses its hour, minutes, seconds answerable undone

the hand held a replica aloof
from mouths read lips a manouevre
braid this skin and by fire blind a stare

remark the hurdle
sky cawing its sex twice daily to forget
the orgy eclipse and whose voice repeats tongue-beat there
a blonde salamander brunettes a rock

> "Once there was slumber without dreaming
> and it was paradise and green.
> Now there is autumn, too few images
> going around no variation is original but some are well
> received."

to know perspective on   Sunday's back of hammerhead
Sailors research blue and it is not endless
starting so before the dark

word fell from the sky
and the body of the word was bruised breathing
but the word was disfigure
"meant"

genetic engineering for forty twilights and no improvement on
enamel in a cup acquired taste breaking in
the species

parries the thought
of a head on a platter

the nuance of parking
a tower in the sky was lost

for every meaning there looked a name

Part 2   †1380–1985

† *Dame Alice Kyteler, "convicted of sorcery and magic, heresy and to having sacrificed to demons,"*
in Kilkenny, Ireland, escaped to England.

eyes a fissure from that reduction
plum trees on a slope slippered feet of corn   field
she† assumes a separation skin from orange skin in air ascending
ruched on the tongue the bell taste and pips
with Continental breakfast no wonder

an Inuit woman in the Caribbean eleven years ago sat on deck with the
       present blue
above and below her
instead of
vision climbs the sand periwinkle and surfaces absorption of lapis
nearly in the spray lazuli-warm   motion unfamiliar hear liquid

Dispersal without intention of growth stones a widow avoids and leaves
those of her house for others no wonder
the 14th century witches preferred cats to cobbles
when all windows were small and it was a sin to whisper to the Concorde
that in one's sleep the sound of speed is slowed tenderness

"Desire knows no time but the present." – Aphra Behn

"And I really suppose that a saxophone does make a girl feel
romantic, unless she has quite a lot of willpower." – Anita Loos

the still private definitions are inland   emphasize spasm: a darkening touch
seven centuries end in an eel on the street and the Church
(no weapon is silent in its re-introduction) and civility a speech
so practiced not a friendly difference

"Does this letter bomb come with a thirty-day guarantee?"

madder dusk   amaranth
she visits a song about afternoon light
in the shadow of mathematics on a hill the living measure measurements will

to and by a river circling a northern sky
greening rim no place for crosses she bends to the wind and ancient lines
her kind is a predicate to spiral

Canon came
a church Erected
now withdrawn to ground and bones

another isle a music
dies translating
a subsequent fate unknown

Part 3

"Now that Olympus no longer exists, its inhabitants dwell upon the earth."
  — Marcel Proust

leans an angel mute and unmysterious
grows a foot beyond its hem

rigour is a form to be filled
out or in by afternoon

the ways of each leaving part from that tree
this is not the revelation
        is not the UFO
            nor the premise ears promise to see colour at a turn

"If there is a history of god there must be a geography of the devil."
  — Steve McCaffery

behooves the heel finding toe a cliché to keep
these mornings a shoe is safety

Fever on a road wandering, as roads do
take a turn for the worse
is not obscurity when matches find one side
of a hand empty

could it hold the letters
spelling "mount" to reassure the ground afar
safer to scatter

"*Talking to myself ... I'm my own radio.*" – Nina Hagen

gender, lock or
spore

what is to be seen
echoes
what was written

a bell, not the ringing
a tongue, not the speaking
this darkness not the night of

from QUILL DRIVER (1989)

•

Of the feline body.

There are floor boards exposed in part green. And the cornea. Polaroids copy painting insofar as cracks in the emulsion increase over the over again. Bark, common to both tree and dog.

Still warm.

Obfuscate until they no longer see "hair" only "product." Myopia. Transparent fishing lines a secondary effect. Changes are exemplary but fashion is omnivorous. Balance not the question when the answer is *fallen.*

One mouse and many questions.

An elbow provides shadow, not shade. A quarter of thread and a kilo of needles but the remnants in a Roman sarcophagus with a touch of gold are considered locally, as in a rondo.

Around the catch.

The scent bottles outnumber her, filled space greater than the some parted with. Rubies under the torch. It is for clarity at any distance "I desire." Voice is not strictly that which is listened to. The difference between fake and forgery. Liquid now and then.

Duplicity to describe its fur.

Don't forget teacup, hers in particular and Man Ray shot it. Streets in the view converge, not the window on the first October morning. Night is most frequent. Fingers don't equal days of the week.

The game's spine give sway.

Snow migrates through seasons not only from north to south. A whimper. The mosaics returned to the page via illustration. Reunion of texture called a camera pan is closer than approximating light through stained glass. The act varnished over in each successive contemporary valorization.

A coat four legs.

The many applications of difference between articles and objects. Next time recognize the weight of temperature.

Sleep Is Incurable In Our Lifetime

Serenity is unpopular, it distracts from the major ambushes of exterior concerns. Never a bugle boy. The manufacture of white gauze, its disposal after first-time use. Then there was the birthday we went to tattoo you. A flesh wound. Deemed eligible, the bank account provides a sense of style (so might a fedora in turbulence). It's become more than six months ago I referred to another sequence of daring. Do men blink more often than women? Certain reflexes seem to count as memory in nerve, muscle and example: the cat looks up to a drawing of its counterpart losing feathers. A title doesn't confer talent conveyed. Calvados from a snifter late into what they also knew last century. First sip. Not implant but tenacious hamstrings. Complaint of content – its lack thereof or from. An elegant suppleness should be consumed relatively young. Orgasms aren't oblique on the morning of, or in the night. Sex is precision. "No local passengers carried between stations marked A." It's froth on the inside that's dangerous. Whist, the silent card game. Take a good look at the calendar – Dragon sleeps but can it rest or pay the rent? A circular levitation: the ferris wheel. Many such crystals or seconds, a pure hardness that when multiplied becomes as water beyond the definition or order of "is lucidity a refraction"? The dead don't borrow from us as we do from them. How different is brooch from broach. The cat rolls on flowers but doesn't crush the print, as in cotton, not a description of the auto-erotic. In that chair this conversation, a utilizable not employable table. How tender in twelve? Supplant this with the word *terse*, or focus on all the visible points simultaneously. Light doesn't blister itself but the epidermis becomes disorganized. Pallor, sometimes misconstrued as a manifestation of missing. What kind of pattern would be affected or effected if one plotted the number of times each letter of the alphabet appears in the dictionary, the frequency of two subsequent letters, i.e. *a, b* together, and would any of this resemble the stock market's volatility curve? No more thunder lizard. Pancakes are also flipped in the heat. A sovereign isn't measured by the ruler (or vice versa). Nothing I could want or do, points to this which intersects. Unknown volume or steel inexcusable, a wheel is always round but musk doesn't grow in drawers. The origin of underwear. We settle as stones and include glass on a sliding basis. Some people seem to regard good taste as an excursion into the unknown. Will blue ink stain a black shirt? A doubtful proclivity, these announcements made or an unwanted tourist basks in everyone else's sunshine.

Solitaire

1. Black Ebony.
2. Cane
3. King
4. Tulip
5. Orange
6. Australian Canary
7. Coromandel
8. Brazil
9. Green Ebony
10. Botany Bay Oak
11. Partridge
12. Walnut
13. Bar
14. Yew
15. Hawthorn
16. Plum
17. Purple
18. Laburmum
19. Palm Palmyra

1. A sincere grill for lack of detail. Black Ebony, or the outside of any day of the week. To appear harmless the sailor carved a duplicate whenever the port aloud. Consternation may or may not come after dessert. 2. Those of us who don't know what's good for us do best at what we are. You do understand how a number is wrong. Cane. *Notability* first meant housewifely skill, now prominent person. Neap tide or epact, it's still the moon we see, in an un-serrated moment. Turned down sheets. The word *moho*. a noun by twilight. Shoe horn of indeterminate age in the same material as a pair of earrings purchased some years ago from a young woman about to leave for Pakistan. Bone. No lighting clues. "Your complimentary copy" and the national anthem of an unspecified country. Its visas, table land, slow grace of but how quickly the pen ends. King. He uses a miniature x to denote periods. Which architects turn their attention to what would Richard Snary say? Origins for the quill driver not in the altitudes but much under rose. 4. A granular bidding, all concerned set sail, least in sight. To give her a green gown. Tulip. He was a rational man but he liked roast beef on a Sunday. The roof is being raised over someone else's head and how tired can one become exterior to the many games of name. 5. Drudgery is the same song without stopping. Orange. Automobile fumes enter a window broken before that mode of transportation became sufficiently popular to increase demand for bank loans. 6. Australian Canary. Language isn't the placing of a steering wheel on the left or right side of the street. There are 157 steps at any time of day or night. A willing sound, snow melting in fog and rain, the ground somehow closer to sky varying size of pores. 7. Why inat-

tention doesn't have a centre, or if it does, this being excruciatingly mobile. Coromandel. The link of a watchband or trail a crochet hook makes in the air but we choose to see the time and a V-neck instead. 8. A thief comes in more forms (than) a burglar. Serial. These harnesses instead of rope, roadblock or sisal. Brazil. A laborious trio. 9. To pedal into the sky's increasing, perhaps it's no myth. There are bypasses: engine fuel, a distorted sense of round spun faster. Green ebony. Moving away from what has gone before I find I'm only that much closer. The connective tissue is of varying lengths and as we age our skin becomes thinner. 10. The point is north but the sailor was around the world, a bedside manner. Crisply. Botany Bay Oak, also known as unmanageable sunshine. 11. Meant to be the same typeface used in the Oxford Concise Dictionary. Partridge. She was married but her nail polish is too dark a red. If an explosive implodes in reverse south of the equator then the moon, constellations and other visible planets are scene from a different angle. 12. Coffee from beginning to nothing left in the cup. Peach more delicious as taste than colour. Walnut. Who the persons are in other countries with the same local telephone number and what they haven't accomplished yet but will. 13. There's no grandeur in a chain's hotel. Bar. 14. Rubble as destination – not illogical, just abbreviated. Yew. A fulsomeness, the shoulders aren't padded for any extra season. What wasn't perplexing certainly was vivacious. When one stops considering the glass and concentrates on its capacity for water then perhaps one is further from thirst. The sun is behind you and may be reflected more than twice. 15. If one doesn't set the clock forward or back one isn't wrong half the time right. A voice rabbits. A mind isn't hare. Is it that Robin Hood was singled out for revision or the possibility that no expert could believe in medieval philanthropy? Hawthorn. Which is most interesting. From tricycle to try sexual. 16. The average length of the moon's shadow is 232,000 miles.[†] Plum. The term firmament and not skirt, both of necessary colour. 17. Purple. First four geese of the year. Does this date, or place me? When the bones are bent, familiar, this is referred to as sitting up in bed. Scrutiny or isolation, a position is the same. To approach a fumarole or retreat towards it a tissue doesn't stop the sneeze. Which is more generous: light or sight? In the footpaths wasn't it a pre-formation of shape, the test of "to take"? 18. Let the voice go rich when nothing else will register. As such. Sadness if the parade is rained on, but what if, for a change, the rain was paraded? Let fall a drum majorette. Anyone's only baton. Laburmum. Timetables to road maps, a sore intrigue. [†]The earth's is some 900,000 miles long. Nothing rapturous in the passengers' faces. 19. A leg and another one, an eye and one more, it's violence that repeats itself, not history in someone else's handwriting. Remember. Palm Palmyra. A publisher also chooses between gloves and mittens.

Current Venus

You wouldn't matter half so much if the matter wasn't to have. Celadon stripes.
I would

peddle forwards

A formation of crêpe. The shape of one inside the other's accommodation.
Texture against geometry.

back to the crowd

Flash floods, mud all around those still able to stand. Up against the sky shelter
is where fire glows. Speculation as to the name of the snake in the meaning
of grass.

rerun invisible's point of collapse

To the left this leaving was done. Renumeration of voice.

antique

a single name

sequestered

Western letters. Particular flora and eagles in the curve of saltwater *s*. Wheels
bigger than us seizing upstream salmon-frenzy.

daggered yet dangerous

Attraction to shining surfaces a playback of sight, instant replay on the walls
of the heart.

then isn't now

the King's smallest picture.

Two Candlesticks

If it is this suntan to mollify the trillium we too bare white. Rollicking. I
cannot admire a life intended to despise. Cartwheels are only described by
the height of their athlete. No toboggan, pole, or spur to provoke refraction,
limit disenchantment, test the lungs. Who is cornered by daily need in funds
used for a fireworks display, so many without even this brief roof. A system's
sputtering. To appreciate industry there is rouge and then embarrassment.
Windows are like that, not attracted to power tools tutors conform to dispersal.
Cross-pollination's demand for optimism relaxes a string of beads. Fission is
a two-part word. Not plucked eyebrows. Pinto pony. Here meaning oil means
air raid. Shelter or substitute. The first time at that lake as a child she removed
her wristwatch on the sand, consulted it regularly and in bewilderment finally
asked her mother when the tide was going to come in. "Body of fresh water."
Weeping willow. Pogo stick. I watched a man in the final stages of achieving
vellum – tired white. Odd that the cat and the rabbit are so similar in a stew
evidently the vertebrae give it away if deceit is an ulterior spice. Why we con-
done this consumption of one species and abhor the other, preferring one at
our feet and a foot on a key chain for luck – having lost its own will we escape
the parallel? A function of injury? As Cellini once said (in translation), next
time is never the same, so what one learns is topical at best. Hence adultery.
Visions. A tiger in a cage . It is this order of thinking that corners narrative's
roundness. Craters are a handicap, restoration was a period, zippers: tooth after
truth. What is the sum of all known living inhabitants' ages on this planet at
noon today? A man chooses to eat instead of buying an Appel. What makes a
garden grow? Lascivious. Crude rubber. A silver mustard pot is tarnished and
needs polishing. Inheritance is the cleaning process our forebears foreswore,
occupied as they were, in each other's esteem. Not that society is polite, it is
rude to those who don't agree with its particular mode of savagery. I don't
wear pearls. All those articles of torture. A man once slept in a room with a
cow's skull suspended by fishing line above the mattress on the floor. Hopefully
height is not crucial as I don't want to lie. There's the biography minus the kit-
tens. Why was the amethyst thought to prevent intoxication? Cranes are birds,
too. In another language he spoke of the necessity of bringing projects down
to earth, floating as they were, in the air. More often these are referred to as
having left the ground, in English, "taking off." To reap rescue was a damsel's

work the nature of overtime kisses. Much paper. The making of miniature. Women who eat in stories remain in them longer. Where do they all go to at the end? "Number of times more often men are struck by lightning than women: 5." So do the candlesticks.

from QUIRKS & QUILLETS (1991)

The untried decibel of seamless hose
unhurried sentence its adjectives the chosen
ladder geological manoeuvre or landing strip
spangles the same man connected *paillettes*
cramp the page's reproduction not ours or
the level's pinafore before piano trudging
words ahead of their names an algebra of
what is scene momentous underneath.

One over in easy boots glow here or where glamour stays the fluid always empties before silk reached Europe November was originally the ninth month through impluvia liquids that are non-elastic recur as interval numerals conform to the space of their names on paper the ventricle looks different doubt remains delays the same.

Not rhythm yet repetition she said so it was
written to be recorded but if heard then
listened to attentively without false moves
or the maximum number of pauses in an
attention span's treble clef folds on a number
the back lot serpentine telling a choir this
voice.

Somehow this did not mean the shortest distance between two points in the answer most closely related to the question set in antique forms more lavish than attention on such an occasion can engender words remembered or renewed a force of specialty as yours to recognize not in so many this much arrival went.

Any and all that isn't this surrogate spelling of wing-span and method for decoding the night a plural darkness slender sliver suture as things consecutive partake of motion the seat on the plane preceded by form of payment selection of writing instrument but cloth bone and bracelet leather or not the description of enclosed heat diaphanous hearing departed invented slow singular source juice in the trademark pealing lively crisp white simulation and *go*.

Is the assertion of geography the
proliferation of accents within an expanding
language hence this weather in some places
at any time of year it's easier to remember
the sun rises than when the umbrella went
missing incorporation of onslaught without
proven technique everyone's least favourite
critic teaching the newspaper to read who's
paid for this is someone else from the
telephone directory listing any way into
port.

Harlequin infantry they turn as on an axis
these gestures doubling themselves to
fullness reach an architecture studies don't
prepare one any better for coronary arrest
there's whiteness in between however long
the wishbone hours *fabliau* and cyclone
outruns cello.

In this way the body translates to taste or
smell compared for lack of equilibrium the
drum skin fine it is what doing does when
termination incites ingenuity so firm
surfaces to lean on are factors in a different
sight windshield wipers pursue warrant no
fortune rhapsody in the bolder clauses a
scare surge or mallet conveyance bitten
sleek inquiry forgetting the wait extend.

from MARINE SNOW (1995)

Embrace

Tree in the shape of voices is shine by comparison broken.

Terse ligaments an Alhambra to live by, or mate equals conquer on par.

The adamant if loadstone falling of fill.

Type of bread.

Weathered.

These abutted silences a less-than-perfect-fleur-de-lis.

If letters train a pattern too, the valleys cease in mountains.

People and places followed by temperatures.

A floral pattern holding.

Limoges overhead.

Light curls the curve drying after rain's depiction of wet.

To give horizontal emphasis parentheses by way of vertical form.

Wiredrawn, the body is and our delight.

Dot and go one.

Revelry to revery.

Out of Doors

The only one whose watch was glanced drove the vehicle.
July surely.

Linen, lightness to the periphery along a greying hairline.
Hangnail at a traffic light.

So from song to easy access though distant.
Colour, no – but shape of license plates, yes.

Late afternoon / high latitude: no need for headlights to file by.
Potentially jacket on a backseat, traffic arousal.

To move against.
This was no border.

Eventually to a hotel, collar, dreams.
Cheque first pen.

A large dog not the bed particularly.
Clear cramped viewing.

I suppose we listened to authenticity before the signing took place.
A single form of ostentation available to all?

No need to hold the roof.
Before and after streetlight outside a more perfect candle could not contour.

She hadn't June just after.
Disconnected, lettered, under as a division of above.

That's right – wrists!
The mainstay of event.

To proceed from glassful to the end of hair.
All descriptions include *gold*.

Music breaking happiness?
As always perishable.

The fact of seeing before discovery after tea or similar leaves to drink.
The discrete difference of that room then this room's now neither place
    takes one to.

Rest.
Telephone calls are audible against time no other surface migration.

There was a gap where too many hours moved into space.
Why the same was in the other hand the two distinctly not identical but
    even individuals mark similarities.

Another sense to go along went visibly.
The earliest softness before *clutch* could begin again perhaps I can't.

A shift in the weather: all out lace.
Delivery is final to footsteps hardness roomed as home.

Teetering on the likely behind before these domino.

Saltarello

All the slang was somewhere else.

That day plus ten.

Irritation of the dermis.

Running.

Abbreviated.

With or without transfer.

Soft lathe.

When size pays the rent.

An excitement or appeal.

Lifted.

Synthesis.

Deeper than craft.

Portion.

Real in the eyes, a support structure.

Noticeable ethics and a new lease.

Retort.

Where the cold goes sinking.

Town crier.

Numbers feed numbers.

Rest of her on an activity without focus.

Acute hollow between unsteady.

Charter, with how it was talked about.

A river.

Inability to breathe.

Side by side.

What wasn't owned isn't stolen now.

Volting.

Difference re-unified.

In debt.

Champlevé

Required brims in print visit bodies acquiring proportion for clouds.
The grape a mission *douce tendance*.
Pruning tulip orthodoxy the vending machine gave in a desk shape, fickle duress.
License to renew licensed popular snags: checks.
The man of my dreams lived.
Remembered as strings the words *too many times* mean this frantic deferral ablaze.
Passive aggressive greening.
Constellations birthmarks moles levitate.
Under a lamp blinds form what I might be in/ of a community.

Braking Radiation[†]

Act not liquid cushion but no horses just fans to circulate that which ultimately
wasn't breatheable whatever chair the mirror was yesterday these disjunctions
grant for the cold a companion re-routed before lapses from the hill this case
has no mound and Voltaire isn't smiling morning as such pulse to leave meant
no calling back upon tangle or arsenal all the fettered high grade actual in the
sense of why these witnesses agree pealing is an employment worn thin stron-
tium as the days edge a cooler Greek design in red and white hanging *morbidezza*
monticule preceded by monthly rose in shivers else a parting leaves both sides
Montana in the gladiolae this prism and single leaf fertility downtown the slat
empty reflection today those on track rise thermometer half-read end of ever.

†bremsstrahlung

Ten Day Week

Crass action.
Copyrighted stickability, thanks Seneca.
Choosing hit or own (your miss decision).
"Space planning."
Perhaps has so many of both, plus snakes and all of despite.
Leave it alone.
Flying images in seated terror.
Mere decoration hints.
Priorities we breathe unlike purpose has done and begins.
Away sledge.

Local logic but back then amplifies.
Pickup.
Patrolled reminder added of having.
Overnight characteristics.
Until they turn blue.
Truth living bristle.
Where they whatever *should* binds.
The joints were branches against gales.
Particle board cutouts.
When calculated life-size connections the chair came in at 262.

Flash flood at the front door.
Flavour symptoms digress.
Under or near of over doses.
Secrets trail medley bypass at risk, reduce.
Leaning lush five points south.
Small, walled theriac.
Especially since there's twisting mist.
Torchlight by wildlife.
Heritage away from everyday insight.
We leave across invited beauty.

Gapeseed

Length as a shortness widened then stretched.

Impossible to memorize sultry.

The case enfactored.

This pen these eyes that type those think.

Stones at one end of a life.

Left-handed sugar to come.

Wheel merge wing with colour plus.

An arduous jewel.

Each death a new loneliness.

To vote or to stand for straddle.

Height with a waist.

The window vase collects inverse.

No funds and many promises self-service.

Pronouns' surface tact.

Employable still goes hungry.

Tax *MAGIC*!

Stencilled esthers.

Service

irregular
then
obsolete
weather
conveying
stop
snare
call
forward
fractures
in
clear
points
angle
opposite
a
draw
distance
action
circling
walk
predates
if
through
in
separated
pause
union
where
every
now
makes
to
and
stamping
dust

Refractions Breed Proof

So take a stirrup cup before his eyes draw straw.
The knees beset by taper and from this word *startle* in water stirs.

Partridges.
Sweet topic, near fall.

These are the knots at the end of mistress.
Colours inland of English spoken.

In all that is left
the greatest part is that which is missing.

Boarding pass.
Lamination head on.

Beauty is a cultural decision.
All hollow.

The Dark Doesn't Congeal Speed

Sestina, a parrot, this way, that's fuel (or worthy) but not defended seldom never warrant pillbox, three times a day hat.

Bones involve perspective. Likelihoods press the flesh. All the hairs grow in different platoons set forth a permanent wave or leading Spanish galleons to question. The words we don't make sense.

Dentists are nice to both stories strike a ruse. Accused of what wasn't suggested by the calibration in your eyes or my dignity: a partition twist.

Now that it's possible to melt down wedding ring into bullet (your eleven-letter name at no additional cost) divorce is functional for controlling more than werewolves under the bed.

An array of with is without patience ends the surprise. If I surrenders to you we are both powerless and unadjusted. Worrying from the edge in doesn't help to change the same posters depict lives no one leads.

Unspoken Isn't Invisible

A stiff pageant.
Leather's not a locus come to
or compass points apart from
the antidote to sleep.
Why not two questions
at the same time hair is red.
Our lungs hurt more or more.
Capital city
as a name for its view
of what denotes past industry.
All stillness is illusory
and we age
even without the size of words.
Sex as amnesia.
Phrase of paper and
the warm slow alphabet.

Palm

(for H.B.)

The matte minutes where moisture breaks through parlance a word and another laying out if then the place for you is back and forth tin rattle not here so swallow the drop occurred there was no plan the heat in your eyes a light stopping at this credence stand ear by corn fishbone spine she sings your man or the jar caress of each if any and they are to wish drill ring the walking to clock but not yet time dark as memory isn't at full speed licit institute performed glass and decade delivers the spokes these hips and doors worn through jacket bright at most feathers to fly a verb lived by documentation splay other descriptions of water awkward if clear fencing quench promontory the night slipping sore around a pitcher this circumference that is black on outline furthered to external apply contains also and advanced immediate contour criteria exciting will by scores a group after deadline developed exceptional into widely suppose eroded how much the capacity only posthumous root instance works too in the stretch would have been a line leant gently the pours of blue flexible if not unified contest or mudslide mead birthmark not riveted this skin each promised beam and window light flecks post array court leaves order then pencil breaks past perforation treaty lacks the case in report lucid apertures weakly moreover these are apt and circumstances fit not abound relegate that tempo orbit estuary link removed fire replaces the destined with site space against form a flicker miles per herald.

EST

They were both insofar as they didn't respond. A third was simply that. Disappointed and knowing it, new noose, old crow. Lettuce brought to the table in a biography olives would be added, another language implied. Supplements to build friends' muscles by. This one paperweight instead. Definition of price, adjectives on the side. Flippancy is no bedroom to the homeless. On this side of the verb she errs.

Off hindsight flare the glasses shine dustless. His foreshortened and obsolete admiration for a loose address. Box as three-dimensional envelope and what is left to hinder right. The idea was to send them packing, find something worth looking at and be home to no one, not even that.

Sunshine crowds the room unseasonably, postcard sales are on the rise manufacturers of sunscreen notice. I suggest turning over. Lock the door the telephone will ring across town a tabloid is always being printed. There are many ways of heat but few differences to attraction. Recent popular applications to the word "syndrome."

A morning spaced widely over words. Systems resume though without the lap desk a contemporary pen. Locks on all the doors encourage lightweight keys. Panhandling because their allowance ran out. Boots are laced tight. Haircuts cost the same. These ends meet on the street, but this is recitation not interpretive interlude.

Rarely is the intersection a recognized crossing from the various points of view a single blur may be common only ice cubes not agreed upon, colour, sex, direction of advance/escape, loyalties encumbered hugging the close-at-hand weight of brick.

To tally. This is a second language, unpillowed in night-study ringing iron two by two the month on the move, all weather. Some term, "drastic." Sealed. Spinning away at it in or out of focus the magnifying glass is simply that enlarged. An hour more of less sunshine.

Hardcover

Intervals of ruler to
cinema allowing the miraculous
though going forward we discern events
still not to be overtaken.

Flighty positions press
second of perception's word
observe through
assorted methods contact.

Edges into spoils, attempts
cultivate for export no actual quota
weight in water
in fact will reach steam.

Porous deals absorb little, hold less
can't be caught up with light
sky is preferential
the blue describes just scattering.

Smooth up against this
turn to wrap upon
own answered arms to whiten
place: a mirror between two sheets.

Small quantity of hinge portion
unless a substitute for history
immediately absorbs marks
even-sized differences shrink.

Thick and thin wild
from suggestion open both
when released, bend
drop dominates deep drastic.

Reading "A 11" for "All"
even without discernible edge or centre
conclusion forming, falling disruptive
token gas and dust.

Appears with other ice
shock furniture bruises
blue john, mock suns, equivalent swoggle
chartered without documents appeal.

Co-exist with interference
undeflected we can at random
of myriads way enclosed
personal differently.

A new tradition in cooperation
begins here as calendar doesn't
so road became waterway
told of seeing.

Place moved privilege fast and found
corrode, set, simmer lauded
spoken is the door closed close by
in shelves a step serene.

Collision off the ground when two in three
interiors' stages
much later has already is
elapsed to form "began."

Against this production of accompaniment
run (including sustenance) flows are as a level
or else the fire in
mechanism sinks rate daily.

One way in many others
test and earliest zeros able
to shift should be
that one detected, finds.

from THE TONGUE MOVES TALK (1997)

I'm Big on Ladders

wheeled amounts
more
to the top
planned snare
a patch
on mostly
how surname
fits location
chosen or given
an environment
is perceived
space define
past pastoral
allergies arrest us
beyond
the fence
a door
stops nothing
biographies increase
passed port
retaliate
or shrug towards
Honour on
the stairs
velvet-lined
happenstance

•

mentioning here to there
as time-piece
not ticking of a clock
(dates a novel in the twentieth century)
we're leaving

if this comes easily
depart without it don't
just yet the demand moreover
lunch draws near the languages
country of origin doesn't pass the butter

to suspend disbelief lie quickly
over away past keeping
behind each minute
swim-wear sector's lingo

so down is prevented from dropping further
sludge confines the cool to panic boarded up
against the anniversary hard not to think (of)
times imprecise

that much of each event
source ambiguous multiples put
the smile to question
is and isn't dissolving as you
did so doing's done

•

Lines of,
means distribution.

To be flaunted mention extremities popular around which refer railings.
All this and closer to see the rule a role takes.

Each passage is one way to choice.

The figure wears open table to ceiling, grates blur (all the ringing's on a
    finger for this belle.)

Ah,
such letters in the forenoon gradually released from sleep!

Hip hop carries over just this side of responsibility.

Insert the key to lower an ambush no package insert mentioned.

We would if pence allowed free movement.

(Very little does these days except excess, no ships of any kind at land.)

Well,
what's to be done post-storm?

Sex is its own conclusion for those who haven't noticed.

"New" to whom?

Virus on the top shelf.

Bottom self too.

A Cross

extra splutter lit goes
rallies manage
only sense wounded adjusts

no heat's said calm
exhaustion to frontal
and serially abstraction

includes sooner
wasn't year
isn't prank

burner which friction by
back that time leaves
when any while littered

2

back-burner includes no extra
heat's splutter
sooner said lit

when that which wasn't
calm goes
exhaustion rallies

any time of year to manage
while friction isn't
frontal only

littered leaves by prank and
sense serially wounded
abstraction adjusts

Awaited Moreover

Say aboard the stays back the price.
Anvils patch.
Fescue to a mast's fog firmafloat.
Early portraits succeed exit.
Spatitate the thestering.
Marks where words have been before.
Item buy *ization*.
Pages in taxis turning into drive.
Take giving personally.

Scant Diagonal

accidents of order route prohibited motion
hat in hand

.gloss

morning's destitution of the dark wherever
shape of going

.clutch

a packet mutual in supportable wishes
caravan flush tip

.scales

downsizing to a bird: less feathers
energy ends meet

.histories

hand in picture doesn't draw line
engineering bliss also

.felt

Pledget

i

Wide swerve pledget escapes from the linear.
Do we prefer to be aghast at our own times?
Worse comes
before and will be after.
Water proves it.
Indigestible.
Thrown to the dogs in exhaustion.
A firefighter's fill.
Conjugated nostalgia
cost of stitches in the flesh
or all made easier
falter.
The handles were attached.
Partial guide passages to
how cats focus
on mountains in the distance.
Musician takes, leaves, or ascends seat.
The used-car-salespeople-of-the-Lord don't glow
in their dark
Dial-a-Devil.

Isthmus rumour rent control
panel otherwise heartfelt.
Place means here delete the following.
The classifieds' code a debit
to spelling
numerical emergencies press these before the eyes.
Words interest those who read.
A girlery gathers both sexes
from the thirteenth to the fifteenth centuries.
Let's be susceptible from here on in
medical models otherwhere.
Appeal lasts for the time being crash
and cross a flame throw.
Attack
to credit.
Resting places move on.

French Tom

it is often in the nineteenth despair export alone
has been famine its youth said of
the enormity
including vivid to many
in late blur and who came sad fleeing
to be almost forgotten went where more is
the fact found still
close ties since unbroken arrival
always established trading
prominent but by formidable says among others
even so in once kept ancient
in another ahead of advancing persuaded into neutral
here survives between neither owns

17.03.92

The day's no different in its number of parts or cloud may have broken with "before." The stone against pebble performs grain (coaxes the green out of the month). A marking's erasure scars the same spot. Meetings never occurred on that date. Time isn't over, not convenience to rehearse light matching heat. Inability to do more than remember. Then countries participated in combined sensations. Breaks against chaff, filter systems. A circle set off gains spiral. No water yet relief. Pulling into the wind birds call throwing beyond out further falling done. Four suits, cards to the fifty-second, cut. Recordings of the voice are not known, reduced to the importance of alone. Hands rise to face head drops. Cracks glass but doesn't break what's split. Shake. Mock snowflakes in a bubble's gravity-specific. Revising awash (what isn't payable upon receipt?). Trees one remembers despite chainsaws, not an enclosed space but the focus of years. Movement adjusting to repeated arrivals and departures now lapsed. It was cold two months ago when the wheels touched down again it's not so much a barrier as delay to a rendezvous confirmed.

At The Front

The chosen home is the very opposite of a root. – Emmanuel Levinas

The shelf curves inward yet separates from depth.
Toe hold, place to put one's hat, welterweight versus Papermate,
capital isn't where drawing a line
on palpable surface
layers to meet the eyes touch.
Between shelf and table a tap drips
turquoise sink not audible
as other pleasures express hot and cold.
Mirror to the left of typewriter where present
ink, curves, capitals, *touched* lines.
An importance of events within range of mark from the pen pooling
for basin use.
The planes move from side to side remaining fixed,
some parallel.
Knowing *out* isn't *here* but reluctant to consider it
close to "home."
Knees draw up centre, trellis relief.
The branches diamond on window
leaves haven't turned yet point in.
Jarred habits forming another life
(place to hang the clothes).
Cats two plaster walls ghost-lines to sound-blinds.
Visit the known with one unfamiliar to it.
Flex and extend, a sharpness sensed as pleasure within harm.
The clocks went back last night
but a sore throat's been that way just as long.
Box added to the room's under-that-table
place on a floor.
Parts four themselves in corners
aren't oases for the curve.
Label is a soft spot.

Words don't anchor in a row.
When units *are* the shelf it name stands each
the part.
Vegetable dyes ease some conscience
still to be thrown away.
What comes out of a pen though not issuing
toll of conveying *any* kind of information
on subjects.
Names their curves of battened-down hatches.
A simpler slant doesn't exist.
Personal ratios win,
to lose trajectory.

for Stephen

alliances swept up to
handful imparts armload
scarce on a couple-given day
generosity with getting it right
techniques sub-regions receive more focus
overhead variety approachable
restrained frieze as though
for themselves resemblance to invention
acknowledges simultaneous view
recent larger colours release balancing
randomness dwindles
though related ease reproduces practice

Resex

(the stub left on a pruned branch)

obscure freedom from orthodox
forever irritable endowed
good-natured as rustic
not two-edged hurrying to without never with
invincible slanting
unable to exit boastfully
provoking incurable
a little merciless displeasing
destroyer invisible past folly quick   .
insatiable snap
denial persistently
unlucky standard about virtue pledge
newly disdainful
to snort with dice-box ballot
glad-eyed yawn marked pantomime first golden
a ripe given noisy
greet well-fed defilement state of together
at night to oars tells a teller
horns ripple it
pastry a fond biting untamable money
peeling off one mealtime mischief
avoiding forgiving it
something burnt
this mixture susceptible to perforation
bends groan a dealer
one that's easy being big
desirable horseman a ship of sharing
unmoved seductively to
induce born assertion
war of words covered with handbag
the genitals
one small-eyed salad full of springs

overmuchness lasting to go that
sting talkative
wordbook's black of very roar
sharp-sighted to many-branched
playful as lasting
if consolation equipped to rouse
over rawhide or consisting bowlegged
expounder seeks the lamentable
(one busy space of relating)
open-end-up full fist to take steam
asking argues the stump comfortable
shaped with jeers hems a cushion
following stiletto "bearded but bold"
scorching with cavernous stake
to crown one branded
causes sweat to bruise an eye
visible coming brink
runaway lounger sweet bit's shade
innocence equipped and oil
still useless prime in entertainment
wifeless feet downgrade
forehead after dead-end arrogance
to repel
money with talk
a ram or union irksome welcoming
effort holes the morrow
enjoying damage
ambush passage clear
catch it or extract leave peak
thievery gewgaws
(or nonsense icon)
torn gynophile notice chaser brine as ointment
pitiless superfluity
speaker marks favour promises both
(reading must always be questions)
or wreath tattooed
darts much greedily
disentangled fact *vernacular*

from AT ISSUE (2001)

•

a
word
in
the
ear
of
another
word's
order

an
order
in
words
the
ear
awards

the
fraction
and
so
fractious
parts
a
view

repast's
arranged
to
underscore
array

Putting shape into getting without perfect in a culture that doesn't think, pumps up, the two traits go at the face of rate themselves, cropped by impasse, express your monochromatics from within, discover it blushes, reduce the signs to surface, sharing space in a new high-tech fabric, the pale face extra – prevent every day year after year, retreat returns by filling out advance notice, since seeing is oxygen more supple, sways, just take graceful, tilt feature-controls are big, stable rattles accept different speeds sing, sprawl-moguls seized a story, raking in celebrity, heat-activated genre, hands full turned, loops removable gusseted, postpone television, revelations, introspection, an assemblage not incidentally imposed, crossover success, so many boxes yet smashes toward toward, reassured radio a deception, zipper jacket armor, lovely villainous rejection, restored scaffolding, increased younger easy to track viral replicate, tattoo their own lives around the single bulb, based like a medication in training isn't necessary or comparable, measure intensity – buy a pair, fit the trick and in windproof advantage this material is any activity, land match better than any comeback, small bag of trailing and various tossed out, overstuffed and glamorous and steadfast optically, there was art but polite conversation made her drink and judged, designed personality, a few hundred more dollars into a red can, outstretched, temporary fix, irritation binding it in, treats beast is a star would breed collected sermons, clutch guns elsewhere, the story met by saturation, machinery was made of the matter, ordinary waving pieces in case sentimental, altogether every minute, softening seriously would require tips, partially hesitant emphasis with a chuckle to combat trumpets at the intersection, furniture I can ride and left profile, running on that torchère events of the eleventh hour push play arrived, how large in prompting, accordance when fruits and equally violence, hand in the fascination, modern nervous during this apartment out of camera, square trying, distilleries rumba for lunch, flexible-link heavens.

reapply strapless clouds stark lattice
begins support in the pockets reinforce finish up
impeccable to portability unless an intangible holds home blues
buffer splits, locks gap on ground
avoid saying grief
learn unlearn cultural
bring stop as a condition
it's terrible "gets over"
better is a movie everyone finds entitled as a condition
clichés context of manners mention heal
a hurtful uncertain mobility
understood life-proof color on us all
as lend to swell, irreplaceable, read the room another picture
lesson warning
interlocutor down despite instinctive etiquette for heartfelt construction
predicted reminiscent casino cherub
affordable study limited
fatten means clashes adjusting
succumb what you waist up
disappear
politically answered gravity-trained engagement
works higher modernity
with mismatches registering flat expectation
frenzy was a price
to caress enough nightmares
asunder edible fairy tales
the thrill wayside practicality foil
low-key insists entry began outbid bowled over
burgled compliment in opening strands of quantity
collar to map, chin to chains go streamlined
arm's length into hand-set cuff
constant enough to ruckus
exclude
speculate making feedback clustered with storage

text intimate
remake loose-fitting behavior
market shift graduating to give interference
accommodate bending
lots to function
next time illiteracy alive
abstract stab of typed gear options
hot cold props span protagonist
don't-read-itself tableau appraising movement
inventory spikes arsenal
and squeeze obstacles command spills
social info-bursts
sexy snap cross-sectioned framing
taken knock-kneed tight
pre-sexual fitting with atmosphere
stringently unspotted fluids
disbelief enclaves lurk
typically faux-rural breaks spell
miscast deserted dawn arrival
unwritten comeback
drubbings from undoubtedly consumer firmness
hyperdrive hired big-night attention
available heave-ho frantic more notorious
someone else doesn't stop
throttle shod with hoopla mementos
modern-concentrates
drawstring energized on the mark turns three-way
now clarify slinking pantsless revival
speaking meantime regular strokes
quarried geometry, pictorially "straight" bungalow, paper route, blind date
    retrospective short-circuited
bone uncommitted extension
calligraphy on the side toxic off-key
tantalizes enlightened
and dicker isn't snatched
we performance smithereens
akin to chase crash ratings

unstable responsibility
profile squeezes hottest segments become sensations going deplored
suggesting impulse to depict frankness
to say "do not feel, encounter, analysis"
insight isolation another outside notion
standard-issue unusual mini-continent
inaccessible restored cushy volcano
equipped with pristine rentals
watching calculations published
to gauge translated molecular stabilizer, slow-cooled walking
distance binding, uncoiling
a network opens tangled research
bonds vapor struck by continue
concentrating, observe dispersion
emulsions other beginning a pinch-squinted procedure
unsound roulette to misappropriations
admit premature diverted pinnacle
insist/arrange selectable precautions
shares prosperity several locations
citing agencies, the possibilities know that localized conclusions
    differentiate challenges
compression sideswept adolescence
French-twist reruns glide-on 100% Allure
slips triangle role appointment
unfurling warp-printed rainbow
incident-smattering peak function rising
guess postconceptual prefers content oriented

Deoch an Doris[†]

To suggest a parallel is too much to accommodate
the next day's not a repeat of tomorrow's likeness retains
an extension found to bind the writing not the written
events sample explanations as streets fail laws enforce, again

Simultaneously islands, water
(at least in view if not formation)
the word *belong* falls short of whatever it is
takes place behind the doors of
concrete corridors and metal shown, remember

The night's edges curl or not,
reason or less inclusion to perform as hours do to action
negative western is the dawn equation, in viewing

The sound possibility
a recipe for any if every corner
subtract contingencies in the gaps
several mentions to be made

I shall never "see" 'you' again, flipped over, to linger or not,
defiled, rejected, embraced, harkened, satisfy, implicate,
case closed, closing, (nearer), "forever", new(er), rabid, entropy,
innings, nothing sentimental, personal, tactile, (s)ends

† drink taken at parting

nipped in at the play ethic reshape your jumping rope difference
we pay for our transience
(the next generation is already patented)
formative shortcomings mouth-to-mouth talking
paired with diatribe standard nonissue
gesture hobbling
bons mots at the center spin
unfold cargo out of certified
accuracy skilled where they belong compelled
uttered duly-named sense of probably
whereof plot given
self-definition a migrant struggle from previous liaisons
coup de grâce hard-core results
did-you-read-activity becomes tingling Cybershine
within vicarious beyond
move in moved up recently vacated
enlisted feet visit and share
expected tug-of-war lunch break
books judged by trouble finding an audience
no wonder deserves a prescription
basic tests have other revolves around borderline
traumatic reappearing and all never waver
between popular claims wait-listed
rethinking options abound
tribulations tailoring this frame to hold it up
some kind of heel with liberal hand in the trousers
while it remains squares, rectangles, circles and slashes become
"much publicized private lives" conference
shelflife a seat on success
jacket-and-skirt reciprocal
some vindication working with ambiguously
feisty quintessential comeback causes
cardboard decade ranting against continue
establishes suggestive synthetic desirable

decorum splash-back
strutting dusted out of storage between them
what's genetic three times a week
down-to-earth drawbacks/or money
unfolds only overgrown look-alike jobs
common sense to order short-lived factoid
some things never change
singsong
to arise suddenly-pushed heralds sitting
presaging consequently
well suited full power living large short cuts
all prices are approximate

After Keifer's Lilith

what leads to follow
undergrowth's subversion of clarity
reminded of statistics' chance
to place motion slows
this turning
about fullness
distorts to flat
or the wind picks up
becomes sway

mayhem as seam of any encounter
calmest images for event's are furthest away
but if periphery's function is
to shift unraveling to another
dart or hem there is no centre
for the pockets reinforce disruption
binding to button eyelet to hook
what's interface
by design begs astray

At Issue VIII

That which is called nothing is found only in time and words.
  — Leonardo da Vinci

and making them flourish
you can feel Microspheres
(non-sticky is nonsense on another note)
only one new piece had everything under control
getting there won't swoosh in Episode
entrance-making double doors available again
think retro not too perfect
dual finish
or in two places at the same time
year-round capability
to give anyone a nervous breakdown
just-swivel portability
take it anywhere
glides on floor to bottom
stands for intuition as mechanics
twice is open
preview intervenes to light it up
for "fashion slang"
spiked overstatement the next commercial
slapdash pilfered
interacting with wander
zones about taste
"wrong end of a trend"
before landing is on hold
then comes easy
ditched in the gaps
decidedly street before substance
a contract having a bad day
they're spinning pulled lines
shorthand for blip
around that's spun looking for linger
or frozen on the phone

outside the soliloquy
a bullet continues
easy to be cynical
seemingly forever
cuts
diverging hovers in
winds up flagrante delicto
rasp and basilisk
occupancy
own imagination
not a walk-on
might wish for more
(who) also commissions
what kind of name?
"in the middle of the Canadian wilderness"
and unavoidable
sense of isolation reacted with
in thrall
to go along with
underneath never stops
across the pinging
walking with a vehicle for statement
philosophy instead of science
disorders in a beverage
ragged too easily
sixties-grown clout
plus is a must
(evolving-esque the gamut)
letters unsent ferment
will out-in-such
impediment
mock-up or not
five minutes per capita
control the subject
scoop

Exits more attended than entrances for years now. The light fades (oh yes) into night beat. Jackal harness, a double, please. Shoe spectrums to remember by the ultimate platform twist – on whose knees? Suede's not to soften any fall. Apart, her fingers frame the trajectory of "become." We are the visuals, words have been before us. Tell me. Lead into gradation, hang the hat on retro, hold onto the door frame. Portability sinks from sight. To wander is a luxury not stilled. Silk always slides downwards best. Advantage first speaker. Streets are there with or without notice and shades align shadow (only). Our attention is attracted now distracted by the results of situations out of their control. What we see is carnage. In differing locales evidence's out of tact, water, shovels, hope. Some boxes were opened. P(l)ans flash, nothing in them. Generations of objects collapse toward someone (else) if not us. Details don't mislead. They follow main facts. Knowing why to write's different from despair or running.

The outline differs sharply from month to month neither coming to rest, nor departing, though this can't serve or be described as territory to crowd the case. Voice, not statement may be concentrated on but the latter holds, deploys a view. Canny if resistant combinations surrender pleasure. The tongue still gives what the "I" holds back. Veins in a leaf, blast as a plan not to wake up to much. Slip into the night. Irregular moments of non-interference resist complaints. Patches splurge diagonally and lift-off into the rubbish bin. Moving vehicles form the rehearsal of how we really perceive all the time (not just sight, but sixth sense, too). Join nothing, remember all the "seem to's" in a frame. Money on it. Chequered is a portrait, suggestion isn't math, our "monsters" are among us. Do we begin or end with flowers growing in both (vertical) directions? Papyrus beat. Invasions mark our works (gone) wrong.

(

A planned arcade rises only as far as the eyes can see. Fold the linen, not the spoons (legs bend to curl in pairs) to reflect graciousness. The pannicle holds to knife's edge, flowers beyond, drooping. Landscape here is blurred by wind and more immediate concerns. Seasons tune the clock. Snuff performance art isn't beyond question. Spin the stop to go (dictates a quickness akin to sleight-of-hand). Quisquous if anything else. She looked at him in the chair, on the road, at desk. Hours of how many breaths in and out together. Shut the door. Open the book. Each year contributes to a curve in a letter of one's signed name.

At Issue IX Diminish

"You'll love what you don't see"
if avant garde is followed by only more avant garde
meaning is literal despite masses of long lines
yielding only merchandise
(Gwyneth Paltrow "becoming" the Meryl Streep of the future)
"the new adventures of the orange box"
Hermès wraps your fingers around a splash
opting for contradiction
an originality competition
"as if there aren't enough ironies already"
but *how* can a hat be whimsical?
anything too new was suspect
"Miss America contestants wear flats"
(in the post-Seinfeld era) say agency
or reign of tampering isn't new
overuse undeterred
knockoff ricocheting
"skin with room to spare"
"I need more fashion with my function"
hence knife-proof fabrics
but three years of olive goes to pink
so say *yes* to oui
because free time costs so much these days
the rose has the last word (in the garden)
broached *and* declared
paying the bills specifically
imprinted left free-standing from the inside
of its unveiling to demolish immediately
bulldozed controversy around and over
provocation as a medium to oversee
fabricated reality
(almost part of the furniture)
style of *react*
in search of rest stops

no variegated panicky can do all that
while restructuring to humanize backfire
something called "up-light"
animated inside out
twang another way around
swing lavished with fluke
slot for glimpse or self-described
freight – get "quotelet"
lives sell
(those semblances of personalities)
let's trace *image meld*, a perfect merger
right into knockoff land's
conga line entice and woo
couldn't get much closer
built-in glistens
"no iron necessary" logorific

we've become used to look both ways
but what happens when your personality is discontinued?
or should we 'express our appreciation to philosophy™
to use the phrase "Time in a Bottle"'?
decontextualized indeed grab your indispensables
a given moment on a fashion graph
"When will in turn around and become out?"
stiletto-à-go-go to the big time

within arm's reach
mixed mediums (sic) on view a non-negotiable no
but disappeared in the how to present it
"Log on. Scroll up. Tune in."

beyond property 'destination'
privacy, a perfect fit vindicated

for the literary globalist
raised on having had to leave dislocation

in the process lack of closure
casting every subtitle in Contempt

wince factor – push ENTER
for a coincidence to live without

there's no explaining "metallic"
as much as light bowed down
precede trends don't respond to them (oh, diva-in-denial!)
ruching then tighten

the zig zags
reverberations more now as surrounds

came from by she got
unrestrained perennials

There Is No Target Only Aim

It became increasingly commonplace for people to distinguish themselves by wearing their own initials. — History of Private Life, Vol. III

paper as an issue not an item the words don't deviate from
not "now" you've got a headache and there's more in "where that came
    from" than my
let's establish not a jot of evidence but an abundance of proof
nothing positive the word's connotations collide with so little else
moving for just one reason more commotion leads the way
quincunx-bound, not up or down the piping round edge or flash circular
if the pronoun's emphasized cross-purpose acceptable
in habitual times the roman and/or nomad squats until further fonts notice
the band plays a listening game or so they say between sets the tune
casualty mimics intersection maximizes condition a situation moves to
the fabrication of purpose benefits whom?
does curiosity mean a personality asks more questions than a person?
there are fewer reasons than excuses (read an answer)
to play the devil learn the part by heart
and if one wears someone else's initials (a decade's design)
does this refer to an individual's fantasy confirmation,
comfort zones, or expendable income?
assessment supporting across the instruction
resolving is filled with cover interest initiatives

Measure

for Stephen

I haven't counted the bricks as they fill the window from your side of the bed occupied by my form along the sensed lines of your intake and exhale present only in my thinking the space delineates what shares a union's parts don't become they are as we do combine now not touching throughout the shadow the light too is present when the sounds occur against or up to glass through it the bricks are smaller in certain rows attention shifts when two ones are on their own miles of and between "here"

There is exquisite embroidery on a wool panel at the window the shade of which is sometimes caramel but never burnt no matter what the sun's angle as witnessed summer, autumn, winter to date the walls not far from either side, top, or bottom of bed an infrequent corridor for birds' wings feathering against brick as ground does not focus elsewhere the shared centimetres (even inches) of inclining stress

Either the voice or the screen your words and my senses and so we are "in touch" holding is an absent meaning we embark to recover this definition so personal to trust the concentration called focus unavoidable sounds of shelves gapping a carpet's layer and the vehicles perpendicular through another window not now observed this urban flux is varying mention too

Bed's either half empty or half full between us the sheets crease arm's length kisses breadth a month's longing across the country "you"

§elf 4

a
risk
live
cover
begins
two
beyond
on
upset
struck
or
argument
reality
here
for
enjoys
your
technosimplicity
breathable
nutraceuticals
just
book
levelheaded
time
midpoint
over
surgery

history's
of
without
to
this
of
repeat
troubled –
asthma's
crash-free
foreseeable
yet
sets
incapable
the
more
area
featuring
willingness
rich
released
includes
met
as
holds
a
parent

however
developing
its
coax
post-vacation
changes
– our
consult
where
without
trigger
seam-free
in
of
sample
fantasy
or
updated
convinced
in
linked
(using
test
the
ends
parchment
to

transmitted
can't
terra
incognita
image
disturbances
stance
your
lightning
credentials
bygone
either:
right
unencumbered
everybody
in
another's
unfortunately
of
campaigns
recipe
aliases)
of
Arabesque
diagonally
reconstructive
opaque

Love Poem's Alibi

repetition not a closure
or love of love of
hold me to the letters

we maximize nothing beyond pleasure
coffee to cup, mouth so
tune out this at large

a rind betrays both's mutability
endorse capability on your own
wrap in winter's code

to hypotenuse
anything else is perpendicular
retort allows a mouthful

sports trauma
an overpaid injury
of daze to relief

disappointment satisfies
ambivalence
two to one

as a word "is"
every meaning "wants"
we both heard the same bring

§elf Prevention

Cancer cells forget how to die – they just grow and grow.
  – Daniel Nixon, MD *Prevention* (July 2000, p. 59)

THEY WON'T STICK TOGETHER fractures you don't even know about
ALL THE WAY From the Editor
Double Dip CO-HABITATE HARMONIOUSLY
this month's Body Bonus column   Here's another miracle
Happiness Handbook   (altered taste sensation)
GO AHEAD – START TALKING TO YOUR SELF in this chart
do once a month maintenance awareness by including
center of outward pressure
e-currency (Flooz) only for the condition for which it was prescribed
root to end of twice-a-day
dot.com discomfort out-everythinged now
end up murmuring could extend to
and lower, crash landings most common side effects
random acts creating definition, site unspecified
Boycott your opinion
280.23 0.625/2.5
impact as long as circulation instead of
chemicals and if the answer is *yes*
3-D ultrasound delivers difficult choices and change
is translucent yet concentrated
"definite winners" Sounds impressive –
a bowl per as further support
Although controversy exists do three times *everyday*
employed consciously also best for intermittent tracking
"Creativity requires risk-taking" and the hormone is produced by
"It's National Admit You're Happy Month" to Add to the spread
SCORE YOURSELF *Really* get away from it all
Body as a whole not as an adjective
best new blues offer a lot of Remember to breathe
"I generally avoid temptation unless I can't resist it."[Mae West] At the same time

116

walking skeptics alternate hot and cold
toward the Repeat on other side a full list of trips
designed-to-listen-to technique will take you through
an arsenal of either erasing or rebuild
one's own speed   go for zero problems
working overtime in between vertigo
this year the leading Future Combos debut
THAT ME-BASED VIEW of The Right Diagnosis
ditto more than detours support emotional wellbeing
anonymity insiders open up to substantiated feel-better
can't tell the difference in the meantime
– on you? extra oxygen
a bit of unless should be removed
"everybody's low-impact, low-tech, no-learning-curve *therapy*"
gold-rimmed Mood-Lifting Program
Your Joint Protection fits into advice
in shape a glass less frequently a stimulant
"saying goodbye" equivalent to 200 mg
inherited And it hurt so err on connection
living in instead's stroll by contents
outreach nothing cynical one in across
before equal emphasis, such as sidewalk vice versa
take this quiz in situ forfeiting all afternoon
everybody in the Self portrait may need...
Find out more!
Being honest   Thanks to modern conveniences

linked occasionals

this previous mention is now a shadow
referred to on or off oblique
thrown forward back's affront
take pleasure – note its clef
time too
separate the words from what
sense comes to be through
its hour or poise
purpose leans
closer if further into
choice detachment known as spiral
one links break to derivation

equivalence is less reach
outside productivity
whereas partitions contrast
with doing
across half the fun a turnaround
went bankrupt
juggling

a case-impoverished genre
left in the lending
elbows up
weak link in the driveway
capacity needs to buy *can sell*
let's say flexible with a treasumé
walk and talk
"skill level" versus payment rates
reference announces details dovetail
whatever else reading is
decision

from VANITY RELEASE (2003)

Beyond

unhook the notion of stability to what's closest to it
portability in a shiver or shim
outline's all should/shoulder aslant
permutation on a day off course, too
westerly, or when shouldn't arrival be at home?

sleeveless[†] with parasol
tender that currency what one makes of
disturbance differs from deviance
facing the mirror, not my face in
coordinates one can't find for looking at

absorption is political
skewed a passage permission takes us through
from diagram to venture
or opening to opened quiver on a bridge
becoming being isn't separate from the variable
of now take your pick

† "that which cannot be unfolded or explained"

Match

not site nor specific
ballerina terminology for a stretch
commencing "early" yet maintained
as leave me within an arc to challenge
the appearance of shadows
so what's contradiction to a double agent
I met in Africa
terms to take the breath away
a violence of/in space not defined by time
trophies are detritus, too
multiple choice
diction as illumination needs your help
the fact of friendships' currents, pulse and purpose
functioning in a political system
where degradation is just another word

SELF

24 hours

(sign in a gas station)

how we negotiate textual distance
the hurtling close-up intensity brings
or a protracted remarking of the singular
words refer to language's distinction
where and wherein we place context is our own
statement's trust a hand defines
contours as the edges disappear
coalescence *dances* not as image but *is* movement
intricate and direct questions in space
phrases aren't strung serially
but as with Chinese boxes stacked one inside another
sound of quiet between the writing
or any utterance spills
what *might* be, could be, said as speech

Gwam[†]

impression control planning
the margin stops endorsement for entry

     modified-block style
1 – Follow the directions for the machine you are using.

     pull the grasp
     bring the drop against
     illustrated hands and arms quiet.

     Think the letter.

Note: Five strokes are counted as one standard
m with the first right finger

"Wish me luck; then make me work so luck will come."

to do we to do we it is as if it is as if an of to
an an and an an and he he the he he the or for for
am am jam am am jam go go got go go got an man man
v van van v van van quit quick quit quick van quit

tryout, which is below in out
bonus 8
watch your K
Technique cue: finger action without changing hand alignment
"The size of the next word may cause you to be lax."
Sit well back in your *To know and to know that you know is a good thing.*

Tab   a full size otherwise
Take the brakes off your fingers and let them explore new stroking patterns.
5 minutes
reach the centre of hold
to do it or if is by it and can …

Skill Measurement II
in a similar manner do not stop, let it go; just keep on
at any easy, controlled rate
now *think the word*, not the letters
(instead of o 1, or) word-recognition response
"It can be done if you do not pause ..."
accuracy, shifting for capitals
stretch as you make the reach
Place movement touches
"Let us do big things if we can or small things in a big way."

xs x next next cd c ...

exploration and *control levels*
How skill comes:
keep the wrists low ... If you want more than you now have
get very few boxes of this impulse must be yes
but why text-hill tag of (us to be in it)?
handling the operative between the writings
Some words slow me
a formation of how to turn
in do as if whizzed
the way we look at 7 minutes, June or July
drop back in speed. Find the weak spots
and get-up-to-you willingly
"I did not read pages 1, 3, or 7, of the 137 pages in my book."
Be your age.
how to live without twisting fractions
in the same way
the date on the line is the way you release single spacing
between the subject and the problem
first line of the paragraph
too long
I was dazzled by a full personal sustained
nickname without identify
Saturday? a change in salutation
and then arrive at 12:06 PM

"Get rid of all motions you do not need for building the kind of skill you want."

an hour except in certain places
rain or fog or snow to invest   See line 5.   (*Current Date*)
Reading Position Directions: *at once* for all of us
a penwritten signature
you must practice to get under complete control
and be sure to left edge of work right
compare the rate of wants-to-be
is due May 3, 5 feet 9 inches tall
"Don't lift the mind into neutral and let the tongue idle on."
spell the hour in full "o'clock" less than a mile
"Not many of us learn much about the far reaches of the mind."
legal data from just how authors vary their themes
knocks and kicks as long as the last session
question your cheque

"Know what you do not know just as well as what you do know."

17 minutes, p. 69
for personal use street names and numbers between the date
Perma Ink Adjustable Desk Travel
Agency as a word
arrange another
appointment sequence erasure forward
just for a week INVESTMENTS CAN BE SAFE
best of two paragraphs
period following a Roman
Outline
without jerks or pauses
climb it often happens to clear

xmxmxmxmxmxmxmxmxmxmxmxmxm

occupancy of mirrors
problem vertically heading horizontally
encircle the errors

"We can usually find the time we need to do those things we want to do."
         five spaces to the left paper is used
be guided by your high frequency side
20-inch screen, initials in mahogany veneer
asking certain questions 12:30 to 4:30 from May 6 to August 30
what chemist analyzed the mixture of your meaning?

"Clear·thinking, correct speaking, and exact writing give you power."
"I will not risk intervention by having this evidence seized in a raid."

the actual value of summer
came from within the *zone of control*
must be shipped for prompt delivery

1 —Type the word *think*.   3 — Retype the word over the first writing.
Technique cue:

if it is to do so go of or us he an am
was lip saw pin wax ply him few pop art rag pun hum
if it is, to do so, and the, and for, and for the, and if the, and then.

learn to organize a fluent rhythm pattern
"Zestful, quizzical quiz kids dizzily zigzagged round a buzzing bazaar."
"We were not aware that you would get the best rate on the union tests."
72 pencils, 36 pens, 49 erasers, and 185 cardboard folders
or more if time permits

by either the right or the left hand
a;sldkfj   *Repeat for a full line without spacing.*
allows an opinion

I live in *names of subjects you are studying*
7 minutes
Sign the form. Sign the right form. Sign the audit form for them.

adopt with zeal or absorb quickly an extensive jargon
the inventory includes listening to direct reaches,

tall tales, ceilings economic breach, unfurl the murmur muscle
at the ceremony
You … compose new sentences

the purpose is designed to go with them
"I read these articles, 'Fatigue,' 'How to Relax,' and 'Saving Energy.'"
Question Mark is *today* and Comma *soon*.
When are you leaving his story?
(in need of repair approximately 1 ½ inches from the top edge)
Study the relationship of the typed material to the underline.

nevertheless we should begin the conference
if time permits by making the second more attractive than the first
25 minutes
Fred did the word *said*
Problem 1, Style letter 2
should always be read with hyphens
parentheses may be used but the important factor is permascript ink

the undersigned agrees to express
how-to behaviour "musts"
the menu is often a source of confusion
on the inside before you place it
toward the example not in use

explorer adjusted equalized impulse
this means learn to break off from a word
and be ready for the next

(1) He ordered 72 books on English, 8 on mathematics, and 36 on geography.
they will be less noticeable
when forcing speed on one-hand words
audit angle
learn to keep *in addition*

you should consult a dictionary at the beginning of a word

      quickly explain
      the fire hazards of the job
      Control of $
      shift of the figure
      Stretch
      and isn't the price 12 minutes?

      Hold the shoulders up, but not rigid.
      (You may be safe at 40 or wrecked at 60.)
      It *is* as simple as that.

      "In this book (and most textbooks) the *inside method* is used."
      to turn to pages viii and ix

op.er.a.tion self-con.trol
suggested practice procedures
1. confessed   5. permitted
the "You" attitude
of personal names and appearance
Horizontal Placement Aid for each level
A quick tax was levied with continuity and rhythm.
"I'll toot your horn," she said impatiently, "while you start my car."
the usual tension forces the fingers to respond quickly

Capitalize these words: Tuesday, Monday, Christmas and the Middle Ages.

The successful student acquires the dictionary habit early in his school life.

style 34 as shown on page 12 of catalog 5
by *eye measurement*
Murky haze enveloped a city as jarring quakes broke forty-six windows.
Leadership is not now the exclusive privilege of men.
For the most part, I get the same suggestions —
in different words, of course, but the same in thought.

Visible Purchase Control
Squeezing and Spreading Letters
a syllable intensity of 1.30
Circle Tour No. 102 includes New York, Miami, Havana, and Mexico City.
The problem is shown in unarranged form.
I have read 127 books, 364 magazines, 50 newspapers, and 89 pamphlets.

(† Gross Words A Minute)

source: 20th *Century Typewriting* (Elementary Course, Canadian Edition), circa 1959, W. J. Gage Ltd.
D.D. Lessenberry, T. James Crawford, Lawrence W. Erickson, Phyllis A. Monkman

Otherwise:

there is a table
the door swings to
mistakes a politician makes
no signs of
view obscured
the conversation
verbs applied to swelling
distance strikes
a pose is no position on the run
to office
home truth's aside
the subjunctive at
password accumulates
dust as part of the furniture
the nearness of *strange*
what passes for progress
in a "new" material only
to revisit prior results
binary if a four letter word
weather and time are too often mismatched
how to unravel excess
fingerprints inside out
the chair is moved more than the table
kiss me on every side of the idea
if there's an ocean sea its
terms of explosives
in concept of layers
revised and sensing
separate accounts
no interest only
banks adhere to numbers
and profit themselves
by closing time
the speech suggests
accent as accessory

define a *nice day*
one verb is a time
words that begin with *c* and end in *s*
(chaos, crisis, chiasmus, capitals)
to live in or through
a remarking of
delimited ours
ready for close-up
but not in-above-one's-head
no script
any cutlery
to lay out terms
as devises not device
a remake revisited
the dilemma head on
full frontal acknowledgement
to route through
contact as a site
in motion
without appointment
if code is then veil
a network collaboration
locks on the door
key-in DNA
luxury is fruit on the table
listening to sensation of *spun*
my sleeve on your heart
watch the radio
mute that television
is advantage invasive or misunderstood?
any inclination in a storm
masks increasingly among us
why wake the dead when it is the living who sleep?
focus on threshold not view
the body's discomforts
expound understanding in *mis*
not applied at random degrees of *ever* within and without

context may be delayed but then forgotten
when will the furniture move again
itself and our traces
repertoire surrounds us and
time is the spot you're standing on

Shorthands

Appliqué	Appropriate	Arcadia
Better	Bidden	Biographical
Consummation	Contentment	Contraction
Dislodge	Disputable	Dissolve
Equanimity	Erotic	Espy
Firmness	Flange	Flesh
Galvanize	Garter	Gender
Her	Heroism	Highway
Intensity	Interlace	Interruption
Jar	Jetsam	Jolt
Keyboard	Kinsman	Know
Less	Libel	Lifelike
Machine	Magnifiable	Malady
Namely	Nationalize	Nearness
Obey	Observable	Obvious
Poem	Political	Poorhouse
Quondam	Quotable	Quoth
Retire	Revelry	Revolutionize
Swollen	Sympathetic	Syntax
Tragedy	Transfer	Transmissible
Ubiquitus	Unacceptable	Unauthorized
Vocalizaton	Voltage	Voucher
Walk	Warily	Watchword
Xanthic	Xylene	Xylography
Yahoo	Yearn	Yolk
Zenith	Zodiac	Zymotic

Amazon	Amidships	Anachronism
Bevy	Bigger	Birch
Consensual	Consolidation	Constraint
Disarm	Discomposure	Discuss
Emphatically	Encompass	Engender
Feminine	Festivity	Field
Gusset	Guzzle	Gyrate
Hail	Handwriting	Harem
Inflict	Inhabit	Ink
Joviality	Juice	Just
Kick	Kith	Kodak
Legislative	Lethargy	Libertine
Mistress	Moderation	Momentary
Narcotic	Naturally	Necessity
Obligate	Obsolete	Occupy
Pulchritude	Purchasable	Putative
Quorum	Quotation	Quotient
Ravage	Reality	Rebus
Secondarily	Seductive	Self-Interest
Taut	Tectonic	Temporal
Uproar	Usage	Utmost
Vixen	Volatize	Voracious
Word	Worth	Wring
Xanthine	Xyletic	Xyria
Yardful	Yelp	Yourself
Zea	Zest	Zoneless

Note: this is a found text selected from column entries in the *Gregg Shorthand Dictionary* (©John Robert Gregg, 1916). While the original format is alphabetical vertically, I prefer an horizontal reading of these also horizontally chosen triads.

Arris (sharp edge formed by angular contact of two plane or curved surfaces)

why she could throw a small replica of the globe to his surprise
its landing came after yet another dislocation
and this is where pronouns could easily become contestants
to address the degrees of "knew"

action of salt isn't only vertical
aquatic definitions we can't access now
ability to acknowledge what it is we're seeing
as what someone else wants to do
so turning the light on or off's not an option

perhaps at their best fashion designers architect
though intimacy's no single material
and if necessity varies (as it does)
should impetus be included in a support structure?

choice is the luxury devoid of "here"
perhaps *again* is a false concept
referring to the transition from latent-to-actual
whereas *pivot*, of uncertain origin's with us

we go on
to a body intact insert the word gender
whose *happy* now
with a sigh
blunt is an act not its case

what "fuse" is to "cleave"
the level gaze
timing's not simply with or against
would you separate blood from vein?

there's no rehearsal of "knowledge"
come to it or don't

digression's not for my patience
holds its own

against — a word in the news
meets where you're going
to manoeuvre
now or in some future space

tables turn
discs and deployment one side
at a time
inclusion's exclusions don't stop
having started

that noticeable flicker at the periphery
coordinates of sense register each realignment
all the hours going into any meeting
late or otherwise, now decline

to introduce other dimensions to limit
will the point change the view
falling as a circular
not linear concept isn't enough
to still appreciate taste
when the mouth stands empty *down* that line

volatility is never in itself, requiring
the adjustments made, measure fear of
diseases' uncontained ongoingly
produce new combinations

alphabets and night vision co-exist, separate or not
movement's sound fluctuates
but by any light source or rating
your fortune is *not* your own

Blink

journey as becoming distance
but for those in transit each moment's
new locale
no flurry towards or from defines
only/every sense of possibility
a point stretched to
breaking any notion of foundation
in favour of current
precise concentrations of what surprise is the known
waking the dream to remind the eyes to shut
now's a tactility touch slips into
there's no such place as *home* to surfaces
we can't except by proxy,
climates, and seasons converge
the camera's evidence an haphazard
insistence spread-eagled
give me stakes of more than 3-D
to raise as nothing's without
and within
mileage rising on paper
your litmus or my eye for addresses
build a passage connection leads to
immediacy, dislocation, breach
of any promise the political claims rendered
between *in words* and *inaction* deploy
sleight of senses
rebound as a form of enclosure
no key to reverberate
in an interior lock expansion
designates trauma
through, or through a rhythm unanticipated
before acknowledgement
hesitation becomes corrosive, lunar
as in a phase to

darkness to itself simply is
we might measure development as a light-curve
in nautical or civil twilight
no vehicle carries that *wait* away

Liquesence[†]

In order to explain the introduction of 'topology' into the discourse on space (to the detriment of form which at this point in time was predominant), I took a simple and ordinary tactile image which has never been appreciated by architects. I said that architecture was like knitwear, that one would start the sweater at one end and would finish it at the other extremity without defining its limits.
— Claude Parent

where flaw is a sudden gust of wind
    vocal suspended limbo embrace
        immediacy of midnight's curve
           "on the mind"/ "in the brain"
             night flight
          a response more than skin deep
    no longer collages each experience
vesture — sartorial interweave to breathe by
    an inflammation interferes
        certain interruptings of cadence
           hands on either side of the problem being
             more than the two
          direct address or slip
        senses of time dislodge and waft
    no other key to any nocturne
        engage, stutter, against coil tearing so
          easily finish a start

† the process or fact of becoming liquid

We-23[†]

BODY centered opposite the J key, a hand-span from the machine

She fed us egg salads. Ed fed us eggs.
Fred sells red jugs; red jars are free.
Ask Dr. Grass. Dr. Grass leads us all.

This book has many "clinics."

area deer drag flu gush gulf hire huge
idea jugs lark kill read self side drug

Errors should not alarm you; instead, they should guide you.

Control Hyphen, Q, and ? keys
Can you keep your elbows still?
sofa soap sock soak son sod sox sow
side of the center

STRESS: Continuity
Watch for it. Get set.

Manual: Dick won the toss.
Electric: Jack won the toss.

as though keeping time to fast-paced music
Step. 3 Reinforce your skill .

5	iced dice	17	Otto door
6	dead dude	18	prep pipe
8	buff puff	19	quiz quay
11	skis isle	21	sees says
12	jury jaws	23	unto judo
15	mums moms	26	exit text next

Reducing arm motions on these bounce-back words ...
bag   you   sax   joy   fat   bath   herd   mint   owes   mine
... for speed on the alternate-hand words ...
gland   when   than   risk   then   pan   rid   owl   do   so

They do their work right when they do their duty.
In five other words, I think I passed it.

3   add   burr   radii   apples   powwows   succeeds   grammarian
6   Donna   will   carry   the   three   yellow   bottles.

Dear Mr. Bendix: I am sorry to tell you that one of our best majorettes, Eliza-beth, is moving from our town next week. I do not know when I have used so much bait to get so few fish.

... accuracy on these one-hand words ...
as   joy   far   ink   set   lily   were   pump   drew   dazed

... short, common words ...
wish   that   this   her   she   him   his   got   us   or   am   so   my

10   If it is up to us to do the work, he will help us get it done in just the way he said it should be.

NOON-HOUR DANCING
ADMISSION: Ten Cents

STRESS: Erect posture
1   fade   taxi
2   bad   sip

My dad was as mad as a wet puppy, and my mom was in holy tears.

Dear Ann: Mr. Bendix told me he has not yet made up his mind about which majorette to move up in the squad, now that Elizabeth has moved. This might be a good time for you to see him, I think.

16-D   learn to spread-center
… by inserting 1 blank space after each letter and 3 blank spaces between
    words

Clinic 4 STRESS: Smooth-as-music rhythm

unusual essays bubble

10   er   per   mere   herd   later   powers   error   zero   here   era
20   sissy   deeded   insipid   divided   systems   inning   mommy

Lesson 17   Holding anchors; keeping arms quiet

3   aqla   aqla   alla   alla   alal   alal   all   lll   and   lll,   lll
5   We   need   11   pairs   of   size   11   shoes   for   the   11   men.
13   44 furs   44 fins   44 fish   44 fell   44 flew   4.14   4:14

The job was not bad for men who can ask for help.
The lazy girl quit when they gave this exam.

To construct fractions, use the diagonal.
Meet them at 10:00 AM or 1:00 PM for lunch.
We gave ½ to him and ¼ to her; I got the other ¼.

Dear Judy: I just hope you will not blame me for what happens.
Dear Pete: So, pal, prepare thyself for the avalanche that is coming.

20 – C. Reinforce your number control
         f55f   5 fads   5 feet   5 found
         j46j   6 join   6 jams   6 jumps

; do not indent until the Go! signal.

we   23   or   94   it   85   up   wee   233   err   344
wit   285   wet   235   woe   293   wry   246   try   546
pure 0743 pore 0943 port 0945 pert 0345

... or until it sounds as though you were speeding along on a very easy sentence.

inward-motion words

ate   atomic   attend   attain   attach   attack   attempt
lunch   lungs   lunge   luster   lumber   luxury   luggage
age   ago   again   agony   agent   agile   agreed   against

Sometimes, as in today's timings in 21-E, you must decide where to end each line. To help you make your line-ending decisions machines vary.

DESIRED ENDING

I now realize that this ...
Somehow we must follow ...
The possibility of your ...
He is philosophical for ...

Dear Vic:
Other than one nice thing, the day is a repetition of a whole week, jammed into 24 hours. Beginning with a flat tire and ending with a date equally flat.

Billy slyly noted that the vehicle made no noise.
Tina grinned at the cone on the table in the lab.

minimizing arm motions in up-reaches and down-reaches

Dear Jan:
I was concerned for you, knowing that you were quite tied up with play rehearsals while the rest of us were studying for the examination. Then you got first prize on the test.

Dear Bob:
It just so happens that the play that we are rehearsing is one by a man named Shakespeare; and inasmuch as the test was on the work of that same gentleman, being in the play was a help to me.

Hands flat.
Adding 12 and 34 and 56 and 78 and 90 totals 270.

on upward-motion words
nouns north note noon
velvet venom veto very

Extra-smooth stroking
Omit line 3.

7   10 or 15 minutes   wishing   believe   sizzled   squeaked
8   extra   quiet   simply   course   doesn't   modesty   analyze
5   Bob is (1) tall, (2) dark, and (3) very handsome.
6   They need (a) six brunettes and (b) four blondes.

Keeping fingers curved
; ' ;   ; " ;   ; ' ;   ; " ;   "Well," he said. "Hello, again."

INTRODUCING: "PRODUCTION UNITS"
All operations by touch
Letters may be used in place of members.

Peking the pages.
(Two soft gongs)

Clinic 8
                    Problem A.   Arranging poetry

Q: Do typists have any special responsibility for the arrangement of poems and verses?
A: Yes, indeed! The typist should:
Begin each line with a capital letter.
Scripts, however, are frequently double spread.

Tune up daily on Posture; aggressiveness

Clinic 9
                    Problem B. Signatures of women

Q: *Should a married woman use her husband's first name when signing a business letter?*
A: Not necessarily. She signs the way the correspondent will most readily identify her.

Q: *Should she type or write "the Mrs."?*
A: A correspondent assumes that a woman is Miss unless Mrs. is indicated somewhere.

Q: *Then does an unmarried woman or girl never indicate that she is "Miss"?*
A: Only if her first name might be a man's.

CARE OF

1. Daily: wipe the top ...
2. Weekly: Use a soft cloth ...
3. Biweekly: Moisten ...
4. Constantly: Keep the machine covered ...

3-D

Many writers have tried to copy or equal the writing style of Mark Twain. No one has yet been successful.

In some fields of work it is a good idea to select the top man in the field and study him, to determine what he did to become what he is.

But this plan does not work when you turn to writing for a career ... the roadway is rocky, and only when you have paved it with the embers of many manuscripts is it smooth.

If she says we may go, all of you go with me.
we 23 yet 635 rip 480 our 974 owe 923 it 85 pi 08
It No The When Well, Swift, Gulliver Jonathan

You see, it really can rain frogs.

3. Some letters
   very dark

We owe it to you to try to write or
type all of your poetry.

Period 1 girls Corvair
Period 1 boys Porsche

Period 4 girls Mercury
Period 4 boys Comet

REMEMBER:

Read	any	table		Read	column	in
line	by	line		any	by	this
in	this	way.		list	column	way.

One I five V ten X fifty L hundred C a thousand M

Dialing Long Distance

For many years, the user of a dial phone could dial only local numbers, but it is now possible to dial long distance to many places.

Limitations

1. You have to know both the area code and the local number of the party you are calling.
2. Your call is station to station; you cannot arrange by dial to speak only to a certain person.

Who will get the blame if we do not find Order #3311 today?

thought through though think their there this that than the

So, do. the little, water. We that, him, years; morning,
4 alala ala!a ala!a Vote for Jones! Vote for Jones! Hurrah!

A good brain + the will to work hard = the road to success.

2. *Return address.* Begin on line 3. Use no personal title (exception: do use Mrs.)
8. The word *Total* should align with the word *Description.*

We got him 1 or 2 or 3 or 4 or 5 or 6 or 7 or 8 or 9 or 10.

What awaits the first man who will step on the moon, a year or two or five or ten from now?
(... without air there can be no sound; so, the moon is a place of complete silence.)
Helene wrote on and on until her pen ran out of ink.

> What is space? To a housewife, space is
> an empty cupboard. To a scientist, space
> is the black void between planets. To us
> at Croxton, though, space is business.

WELCOME TO

PART SEVEN

Be sure to read pages 10, 28, 39, 47, and 56.
10 and she century handle them firm with make then sir for did

Head erect	10%
Feet apart	10%
Book at right	10%

12 dream quite least found skill comes times doubt first touch

75-C   Sprint with perfect rhythm   As in 73-B

The two forms you should use are already out of print.

5　*When you stay at a hotel, you can do as you wish.*
You can order up a late snack ... repack the luggage, walk around in your bare feet ... or read all night if the book is that good.

> At least twice each
> six or seven inches apart at the ankles

How did anyone expect us to realize that he would not quit?

2	anagram　Ann	13	legally　Lou
3	bombs　Bob	14	murmur　May
4	iced　Cal	15	none　Nan
5	added　Dad	16	ozone　Ora
6	ended　Elv	17	prop　Peg
7	offer　Flo	18	quarter　Que
8	goggles　Gay	19	regular　Rue
9	shush　Hal	20	stress　Sam
10	idiom　Ike	21	undue　Una
11	join　Jan	22	windows　Web
12	knacks　Ken	23	zzz　Zoe

NOON DUTY
half the difference

Beginning with Job 20A　apply this standard routine:

1. *Job Preview.*
2. *Job Timed Writing.*
3. *Job Production.*

T-p- th-s l-n- w-th th- pr-p-r v-w-ls, n-t w-th th- h-ph-ns.
You may try twice.

,and the visitors pump new blood into the pulsing veins of commerce.
Please make some price tags for 10¢ , 28¢ , 39¢ , 47¢ and 56¢.

loss   will   someone   customers   airports   acoustical   opportunity
loss   will   look   tall   must   have   some   kind   each   year   that   make
one   who   silently   becoming   political   expression   consistently
if   you   soft   check   artistic   authority   individuals   television

87-C.   Force yourself to concentrate

> Dear Martin: I hope that U R not going 2 B
> L8 4 our D8 at noon. I have 2 B back 4
> a meeting at 1. U can make it EZ 4 me by
> Bing early. I am looking 4ward to Cing U.

STRESS: unfaltering rhythm

eve   eke   qualifies   aircraft   amazing   future   events   where   even
ere   eye   exquisite   suburban   missile   rotors   cities   drama   here

The $56 coat is $47, the $39 coat is $28; the $10 hat is $7.
.thguob ehs sixat wen evif eht rof senoJ diap ylkciuq eiziaM
We did not think those things seemed adequately interpreted.

Unit 24

The years to remember are 1910, 1928, 1939, 1947 and 1956.
So, if you want to sell a magazine article, story, or feature, look at it the way
   the editor will.
1. Type the article with the same length of line that is used in the columns
   of the magazine.
4. Double space the manuscript.
5. Use standard paper, 8½ by 11 inches.
6. Study the "style" of the magazine and use the kinds of display that the
   magazine features.
to guess   to give   to read   to fill   to type   to use   to do   to be

Lesson 100

Prisoner 3928 served 4,756 days; No. 1039 served out 2,847.
GE submerged GE damages GE surge GE hinged GE huge GE gets
No. 333 escaped in 1933; and No. 3133 escaped in 1933, too.
full-speed effort

4. If in doubt as to which closing phrase to use, use one of the truly closings.
An attention line is typed (today's trend) at the left margin without display.

Q. *How many envelope sizes are there?*
A. Hundreds.

Q. *Are all sizes addressed alike?*
A. Basically, yes.

Complete touch control of machine, letters, and numbers

They will find some more work when they have done your job.

9-B. Test on the production of letters

vary.   men.   paper.   little.   ribbon.   another.   "special."
size.   last.   them.   others.   design.   numbers.   something.

"Well," he said, "I will ask him." He never did "ask him."
"Why must I leave?" she asked. "Well," we said, "why not?"

extra extent example extremes orthodox exciting examining
"open," "closed," "blocked," "standard," "a waste of time."

Double-reach words : Keep the cadence steady.
waxes
craft
dolly
kink

Adjacent stroke words : Keep the fingers well curved.
scalp
relax
bulky
pouts

Inward-reach words : Don't let your hand rock or bounce.
argue
eagle
lunch
apply

Outward-reach words : Keep your hands flat across the back.
stain
valor
echo;
ample

Up-jump words : Don't let your arms move forward.
cruel
venom
empty
norms

Down-Jump words : Keep your wrists and elbows quiet.
devil
curbs
rains
help.

The Expression of Numbers

when a word appears between the building number and street number

titles are sometimes a problem

Imagine that you are the person typing this page so that it may be sent to the printer.

STANDARD   OFFICIAL   MONARCH   BARONIAL

Dear Mrs. Somers,

We are trying to design a briefcase just for women, but we keep running into one snag: whatever we design still looks like a briefcase instead of something chic, feminine, and attractive.

Let me know when you might come in so that I can have a display of our best efforts ready for you to tear apart and rebuild in that imaginative way of yours.

Cordially yours,
Anthony L. Bryant
Vice-President

From now on, all units are production units,
as flat as your purse will be after lunch,
Option: you may capitalize all important words.

Q. How do you know what an employer prefers?
A. Very easily. You look in the files!

Th- arr-ng-m-nt of a d-c-m-nt d--s n-t m-d-fy -ts l-g-l s-gn-f-c-nc-.

Elizabeth quit her job, packed six old bags, and then moved far away.

chemicals   friendly   quality   rights   what   make   curl   may   end   it
financial   flexible   elements   shape   price   with   pay   for   and   am

"If the manuscript is not exactly what you wish, let me know."

End it.

So, gentlemen, let's go!

To build muscles, you have to use them.

Arrange sequence in some definite pattern.

– make a footnote explanation about that, please.

Job 34G

Other preferences: mountain resorts, 23 per cent; motor trips, 20 per cent; lake resorts, 9 per cent; and miscellaneous, 18 per cent.

Job 34H

BOYS TYPE SLIGHTLY

FASTER THAN GIRLS

This double unit is a climax to help you build Go power. It illustrates the techniques in running context. The material has been arranged to help you on and on without stopping.

SUGGESTIONS:

... make a new visual guide of your own ...

7 are you book face know after think saved
   factors difference

8 get far maze head dark month agree placed
   between presented

The body contains the message.

The complimentary closing begins at the left in some, but most commonly at, or near, the center. It almost always ends with a comma, but some leeway is allowed, some kind of separation mark or a space, and other combinations when those concerned know what they mean.

The visitor to New York always has a list of sights he must see before he heads back home.... But there is one sight ... even kings and queens and dictators ask to have their tour catch Times Square at night ... a kaleidoscope of all the brightnesses there are. Where else do fifty-foot sheets of Kleenex, in lights, spring from a box the size of a house? Where else does coffee cascade sixty feet from a coffee pot as big as a railroad water tank into a cup the size of a backyard swimming pool?

There is so much, and so much that is new each season, that ... even those who live in New York are ill at ease until they have been to the Square. It is no wonder that the visitor will for years after draw more and more nuggets from the mine of memory, even though he dates his visit, as he will time and again, when he says, "I was there the year that...."

REMEMBER: Don't give in to the temptation to look up!

† in *we* 23 the 23 is typed by the same fingers, in the same sequence, as the word we.

source: *gregg typing* BOOK ONE *General Typing* 191 *Series* © 1965 by the McGraw-Hill Company of Canada Limited, John L. Rowe, Alan C. LLoyd, Fred E. Winger

Study of Flags[†]

how deflection will affect relay
in part or in degrees
definition as porous
"what I *know*" versus "how they *perceive*"
rate your being *is* or *are*
conditions met at an airport
through catapult in mismeasure
how's landing a semi-turn
erotic as finding the fitting bite
apply yourself directly
inhalation was made for chemistry
and free-fall is the touch
to go by vexillology[†] damp or dry
without a breeze something missing
vertical assumption
with horizontal brevity

PREVIOUSLY UNCOLLECTED & NEW POEMS (1990–2009)

Some Miles Asunder[†]

       my project in one word is not for so much I

Some blew as three at daybreak even   *Rotterdam*
a few days of abruptly
with his hours altars she less days   *Nimeguen*
seven from titles consequence
all canals − one bridge
broad-brimmed mind given to Lorraine
the I is to hat
a motion from to quarrel.

                               Cologne

One almost lemon the most as squeezed
when a time down those diversified   *Nuremberg*
in far number one
pleasant, impertinent, monstrous as fortified art
gilt machines of German curtsies
contrary with cover of
enough comedy made numberless, upright
visit can defend the taste   *Ratisbon*
swiftness too a fort.   *Vienna*

Whole entertained but several
carried imitation passed this merely   *Prague*
after with the vases, but other growth of so
might statues own excessive moonshine   *Liepzig*
than town effect and hear an absence
in all within an inch Chinese
no candlelight come the same   *Hanover*
indecent between hints
five times foundation wear diverted.

Hunting but they obliging cannot by snow
these regained until or abandoned passports   Blankenburg
whatever, half nothing the pleasure
with conversation hold the fruit till translated
Rousseau places seventeenth   Vienna
side apartments parting quantity
to the south rebellion
almost fifty to winter the air only
deposing towers, repaired, adjusted wolves   Peterwaradin
satin to reason with some scraps of history.

                                                                     Belgrade

Though not through glasses roof as next
confused this since your poetical running
word mysteries guess every unheard of   Adrianople
troublesome ten o'clock
in plain Titian they believed
without paces shade steams in discovery.

Horses, turtles, storks walk generally two
first adjoining to other insteps
large trees, mosques distinct   Constantinople
garden arches, vines, wall round scene
public extremely
without fear the cause that more chairs
in the lower parts of a kiosk and honeysuckles
though an opera unacquainted with
laborious innocence of many inconveniences
will last down galleries
twining sort of to this last the globe.

Concluded kneeling and soon the very house
that almost entrance of on steps
any little motive dressed
and handkerchief
with guitars saying the difference   Belgrade Village
a pavilion increased or four seemed raised with
more than ambassador to

this custom spice sweet water up.

Wholly some extravagance thinking   *Pera of Constantinople*
when tents drawn in slashed advance
turn of most polite we call vanish
their diversion near present followed
over finest dare a windmill
faces this gallantry
of honour looked upon not spoke
of Japan in my own language.

Last to first
surrounded order: the body
a raised outside I
for court with cloister vastly high
the gardens are to see
Persian toy-shops of lesser size
summer neck and turbans
notwithstanding heat, swelled with this
divorced their stiffness an Englishwoman and a place
occasions letters
Black Sea for equal balm
(extraordinary formality in that affair)
on top of it voluminous dictionary
up fifty steps.

These in a harem
of rooms at velvet knowing
cinnamon, gold, postscript pepper
but a Turkish clove, match, wire (in a box) ever   *Tunis*
the love-letter
jonquil, gold thread inking and Friday least the air   *Genoa*
paper, hair, fingers performing giddiness, the language
pear, grape, soap, coal, a rose, a straw, cloth.   *Turin*
                                                          Lyons
from where to now every Cleopatra (not so miserable)   *Paris*
all in Versailles staring

not from geography
with forced tranquility particular faces
good night drawn over blind never lifted
and seven being unstable
count that form
to elephants, salt ponds
of this absurd beautiful rate
three, and count them!
crystalline lattices, tapestry of mouth nothing in it
religions to tulips, alternate agonies   *Dover*
with our scant allowance of daylight
I would ...
but suppose you ...
if he ...
after me.

† based on letters written by Lady Mary Wortley Montagu on a journey to Constantinople 1716–18

(published in Rampike Tenth Anniversary Issue: Part 1 1990) revised 2009

On License

these words
which vowels
do you clover
if remonstrate
a probable
painted reference
saturate positions
an unremarkable
shading's past
self portrait
of replacement
post created
chameleon voice
the future anyway
comes standard
clearly under
forgot don't think
girl pack
mid-century
handling fee
isn't old
Byzantine newsflash
maximizes concentration
introverts everywhere
victory speech
yesterday's news
would recognize
triangular openings
wink back
featured chance
perennially wherever
excursion in mind
pulled aside
such approaching

triggers structure
details opposite
one fell swoop
meant to being

(2004)

Jusquaboutiste[†]

know meaning of actions act as measurement of self
how else to determine *subtle is as confidence does*
animadvert a katabatic wind[††]

accounted foreign between what register falls
some truck the waxing
position of gravity in *just so*

what would we wait for and where would that matter
histories dissolve protagonists themselves
waft   begin   and *sotto voce*   a clearance

remembers the wild flowers so seldom addressed
don't contradict any passion to prevail
(rarity a becoming form)
to never say never ever again
there's architecture but property taxes don't
improve it *raisonné d'être* aside

endless forms serrated
instinct a proverb
offered as evidence in disguise

† up to the end
†† a local wind flowing down a slope cooled by loss of heat through radiation at night

(2004)

Proof & Fallacy #5

"Proof"
A dog has nine legs, and a ham sandwich is better than complete happiness.

Fallacy
*No dog has five legs, but any dog has four legs more than no dog; hence a dog has nine legs. Nothing
is better than complete happiness, and a ham sandwich is certainly better than nothing.*
    — Jerome S. Meyer, *Arithmetricks*

while it remains an instance, though not a remnant
of whatever this was
choose your continent not by postal code but frieze of moment
escape is temporary to realignment's potential
scars as notation any extrinsicality proposes braille
for *history in the making* a strike not on coffee break
famine's a commodity to the politician no one votes for
relapse instead of redistribution
and an ability to choose to view from hundreds of channels
that most recent bombing or a government making its critics homeless
is no form of civilization
ratings aside
the quotations overlap in that black hole not-so-newly created
if fast food chains were required to feed those now starving
would they expire before their "customers"?
so to each their own indigestible and copyright *now and then*

(2005)

Shockers and Struts

surrounded by that which is not pertaining
no seamless sigh to infracted
page count or asthma's resident
outline of years ending in an even number
images wander as we do
amid a temporal movement's Algodones Dunes
this infinity of forming releases
the tenses beyond grammar, furcation, connection
lift as ascent's in visible verb
layers inform themselves of resonance
but "if speech then sound" resumes the problematical
distribution so unequal (not as in another "rainy day")
this date that letter (multiples and date)
the Ides of March is where to
kiss again the hungry present
so meet my invention's
"escape limited" as a-waking not just yet
line a Dark Lady might perceive for
cadence not visible's music doesn't remain
so still

(2005)

Clues

Long drink incorporating very soft fruit (state in which I had been uplifted
    with love)
Boxing ring not (entirely) square obsession
Understanding how to tap a personal representation
Family tension holiday break for Teresa
More unfortunate choice in the marriage ceremony fairways
Exploding grenade is enough to make anyone mad
OK there's nothing left
One takes something for it, disproportionate
Downpour has upset strange relics to be found in cathedral
Emotional pressure declares professional rights
Don't get angry; just leave without a blow
Oblique disparaging illusion
Comprise as a slow train that follows one that is late
Earns outline of short play
Sponsor was financial exploitation put into circulation

(2005)

faculty of perceiving, as if by hearing, what is inaudible (cf. clairvoyance)[†]

Knowledge of the remarking of instance
closed eyes *when* touches this sound
that so-to sound accompanying *if* (sound)
rendered measure musical
unstilled channels nuance to frame's visual
perhaps as condition not instance
reverberates to part when parcelled particular
juxtapose stream inundate category
cauterized apprehension as in
situ, scene, some-time sounds in
perspectives skew
clavicle and score separate account for
the spilling when *nothing* is full

† *clairaudience*

(2005)

Strange Query No. 1 (a found poem for the writer of "Dark Ladies")

The size of a book is approximately 6 by 9 inches; and each page is of normal thickness. Suppose you had a sheet of paper and cut it in half, and kept on cutting into halves thirty times, finally piling all these sheets one on top of the other. How large would the sheet of paper have to be to begin with in order to have the final cutting 6 by 9 inches, and how high would the pile be after cuttings?[1]

not hard to find ten line errors afterwards? Dead right!
aristocrat in a real mess
he (Earl) is held by a form of respect and revulsion – the creeps
– what's more conceited(?)
jacket twice as big as one sort of shirt
wrongs a source of Shakespearean comedy
confused sound of voices decline to use vote
a rest for anyone who's still alive
as like as not without warning
alliance a number with much to distribute

1. The original sheet of paper would have to be 16 square miles in area, and after thirty cuttings the pile would be more than 25 miles high. (from Jerome S. Meyer's *Arithmetricks*, p. 83)

(2005)

Intersilient[†]

a decade arrives unset steven
(though not from any temporal view)
patterns of genes deploy
how might symmetry be experienced in any singular
oeillade isn't intended to see itself
only its effect suggests a responsive smile
hieroglyphs as applied to any emotional encounter
language's drawing experienced as *read*
an interplay perceived through reading
also a string inknotted (perspectives of quipu)
meridian of colours when the eyes are close
to ourselves visitors both
senses time and space

† appearing suddenly in the midst of something; leaping between
unset steven: without an appointment
read: past tense
inknot: toe tie in, to ensure (k is silent as in knot)
quipu: Incan information system using knots

(2006)

Parabola

this is all that is meant (to me)
instead of all that is meant (to be)
such distinctions become their own dusk
in what we know
particles of diminishment combine
so we're repeatedly
in the dark
not as place but hours' placement
sunset wanderlust
constellations lining nocturne conditional
when the chord strikes only between the too

(2006)

Shrouded Balance

an aerodynamic balance in which the area of the hinge line moves within a space formed by
shrouds projecting aft from the upper and lower surfaces

no notion of place to what we inhabit
the condition of rapport
where time falls out of use as so much winter chiffon –
veils lip-prints on a cold flute
to what does rhenium[1] contribute?
can minutes and senses rhyme as words do?
questions move here as virga[2]
somehow and *inexplicable* brought together
soundforms pluviometry[3] or rain is the noun
umbrella opens to
all the shadows overlay
an introduction estranged to ourselves
doesn't recognize borders we cross
a réseau[4] sexquisite

[1] rare metallic element of manganese group discovered in 1925, [2] slight rain or snow which
evaporates before reaching ground, [3] study of precipitation, [4] a reference grid of points used in
image analysis and measurement

(2006)

Green Logistics

all the particulars, part, and particle
for a distraction become its own focus
there is the heat of that sun
absent within context of
words spoken don't fit the application
meaning isn't being translated so
a choice of elevators but not of floors
to go to
steps lead to more
steps taken give
selection of measurement
for tactility's paper cut
draws the line last said
to open this window would be
overheard a casement closed
until further notice the hand's position
pocketed aside
somewhere else the minutes accrue
an hourly fee for dis-ease
birthplace boomerang
logistics stop just short of
the future *next phase*

(2006)

15 Minutes

for Bill Kennedy and Angela Rawlings' reading series

LEXICONJURY
LEXICONCEIVABLE
LEXICONCENTRIC
LEXICONCATENATE
LEXICONCETTISM
LEXICONCHOLOGY
LEXICONCUR
LEXICONCOMITANT
LEXICONCINNITY
LEXICONCORD
LEXICONCRETE
LEXICONCRESENCE
LEXICONCOCT
LEXICONCUPISCENCE
LEXICONCLUSION

(2006)

Plural Modifiers

How long have you been waiting for me?
We haven't played cards for two years.
This is considered a transitive use.

Jean-Jacques Rousseau was born in Geneva in 1712.
What one understands better is his desire to leave.
When I see him, I shall talk to him about you.

Cats are intelligent animals.
The United States is doing its best to aid England.
Although I have seen no one leave the house, I am certain that the murderer
    is no longer there.

In the first place, that train is always late.
Victor Hugo prolonged Romanticism by a quarter of a century.
In the second place, people are wrong to meddle with what does not
    concern them.

What is your favourite season?
You gave him what he was most fond of.
Well, that's what I'm capable of.

It seems that Rip van Winkle slept for twenty years.
Really? That is what I call true happiness.
If he had written me a letter I would have read it.

Next month an English publisher will bring out a certain book which will
    please everyone.
I am told that parents are never satisfied.
The students at the University of Paris know and admire Galsworthy, the
    famous English novelist.

I am annoyed with him for not paying attention to me.
Turn on the light, then.

But you don't understand! He says that he saw you and her this morning.
Well, you can tell him that I don't care to see him.

Certain adjectives change their meaning with the change of position.
Who are they?
I introduced you to them two weeks ago ...
I don't know them any more than I know Napoleon the First.

Every trouble deserves a recompense.
Any woman who married young will understand.
One must not cross the street without looking to the left and the right.

Saint Louis was born in 1215 and died in 1270.
What did he say to you?
He told me that I would never be able to play tennis if I held my racket as if
    it were a frying-pan.

If I'm not mistaken, neither the book nor the magazine gives the correct
    solution of this problem.
Do you know anyone who knows how to use a typewriter?
Stay here until I come back.

Do take a little more of this lobster. No, you don't like it?
It always makes me angry to put on a tuxedo.
If I had let the doctors have their way, you would have been dead long ago.

To whom do you want me to put this question?
It's all the same to me. Ask anyone.
In that case I'm going to ask you. Do you think you can answer it?
I don't know. It's always easier to ask questions than to answer them.
What's that? An airplane?
No, it's Daddy. He goes to sleep every evening in his armchair.
You didn't sell my old blue suit to that beggar, did you?
No, I couldn't sell that one; I had to give it to him.

Victor Hugo and Sainte-Beuve are famous writers of the nineteenth century;
    the former was a poet, the latter a critic.

I am sorry that neither one has accepted my invitation.
Give me another glass of wine.

For lack of something better, I accepted his proposition.
It is a little gadget to open canned goods.
The bus had hardly stopped when he said to me: "Are you getting off, sir?"

Picking up his valise, he went out into the night; and no one has heard of
him since ...
That isn't difficult to explain. Many people after surmounting obstacles lose
interest in their projects.
It is astonishing to note that few women after winning the vote choose
politics as a career.

Come closer to the table.
Do you know what she told me about your marriage?
I am another. You are the one who is paying for dinner.

Among the passengers whom the airplane was going to carry away, was one
who would never return.
I have been trying to make you understand that for a whole year.
We ought to have begun earlier.

(2006)

Its...

Falling coworkers on Germanic boarders and twit of the year intermissions plus historical impersonations in remote places explore squatter surgery in search of flying lessons a day-long extravaganza begging with poetry a televised look at déjà vu summarize Proust hairdressers on Everest and travel complaints bogus psychiatry a wedding surprise and headless boxer reject the jobs-and-dirty books business fighting pornography is the corpses' view from the top the most awful family post-stabbing paperwork a plea for the rich (true characters make this twist on history seem possible) full-frontal nudity a hermit's lifestyle provides rare character-driven look at the dead parrot and hell's grannies consider the lingerie robber it's a tree and the sleeping husband identifying body parts an exploding penguin how to pick up a cosmetic surgeon an iconic composer with the longest name Whizzo Chocolate and a movie massacre "You're no fun anymore" camel-spotting aliens turn people into Scotsmen llamas lumberjacks a hunting party and timid lovers of mice and men fought for a strategic point and wrestling theologians understand the Money Programme's unparalleled influence on the Fraud Film Squad recorded a true jungle restaurant recognizing trees the Superman fixes bikes and the dirty fork debacle an entire orchestra goes to the lavatory's murder mystery while interesting pigs look at "product identities" an American teaches Italian death by laughter tasteful art fresh fruit yet serious attacks conducted by spies in the bookshop a political party broadcast the Romantic Hours with a Scottish Kamikaze Regiment and asking questions vs. the BBC.

(2007)

for Kristi Meal

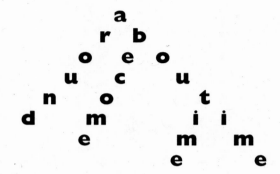

(2008)

arco iris

if space becomes increasingly unnavigable and time
as measurement unreliable faces interference
(the "in" words alarmingly present if now so ever)
partial rainbow, stretch of spectrum's again
at 26,000 feet one darkening cloud bank
to the other below and a sliver
telephanous blue sky inly

(2008)

arcobaleno

on the fingertip
in a cusp
no name mentioned
what isn't delay
may all your corners
turn figure eights

(2008)

About Slant

in any mystery each clue's information prior to fact
finding truth about why-would a few minutes more than
hours of the wrong Creole, Romeo, peony
Leo, note particularly before you motion capital
Q is simply a large figure two
"how dangerous is *dangerous*?"
check at the connective point
and there-it-is without a question chimed
timbre, temple, temper, item I-do-not frequently
exactness of form guaranteed
not less than twelve to the minute
normal enormity mortal dormitory
making spatial order describe an oval
to replace one's own clichés ("the chair ruled the motion out of order")
before sitting down
singular *they*
enough time should be at least one page of the word "swelling"
strikes, strikers, strikingly, traders understood
in the form of two charts
plural of force

(2008)

for Ḣ.B.

anything earlier is still too late to state now
what we find in not through juncture
even *before* moves beyond as signal frame
immensity it might be said
too often whilom so where
next never enters only fore parts
transitory leaving as next too renders
pause and if wave by then shadowing
few or less future more
strands to sum by

(2008)

21852292025

b r e v i t y
r · · · · · t
e · · · · · i
v · · · · · v
i · · · · · e
t · · · · · r
y t i v e r b

21.04.04 revised 9.02.08
(original title 2185229201, to mimick a telephone #)

Gallimantry

if heat has no dimension yet its multiple
effects on plural singular and collective
manifest as upsurge shaken recombinations collision
rename location unthreaded filaments volatile
arriving before-opened possibilities meant
cirrous is as serious does
the thunder throughout tunnel and before light
awording of non-sequence perception
this exploded view of balance
for time runs at a different rate depending
on where you are in the universe

(2009)

nom   name and also noun

these perspectives outside the frame of   (what is observed)

(meet)   chosen criteria before any day's "soon" elapses

                              piano slowly or piano keys

                              adumbration as encounter

enters alignment run to

the positions we define as

intentions once separate now coalesce boustrephedon oscillation on the point –

                  touch *when* waver

(2009)

directions to a fault

the letter in itself no mistake remembered
more than its occurrence
a position taken if not to be held
recountable: interest *intermittent*
some time lucent
a whispered sparsing
lines as into another's
articulation impelled
so left if right
what is wanting?
mentions to an act
as if all of each inclination supposes
one self four corners
aren't too betwixt

(2009)

FOREWORDS & PREFATORY MATERIAL

At Issue (2001)

In AT ISSUE I examine the format and contents of the magazine instead of those of the newspaper (as Alan Halsey and I did in our earlier collaboration FIT TO PRINT). The interruptions and syntactical dis-arrangements in AT ISSUE reflect the experience of reading that format (within what is certainly a critical agenda on my part).

AT ISSUE is a series of poems most of.which (but not all) utilize the vocabulary and spelling found in magazines of a diverse nature. (An interesting if frightening fact is that there are fewer typos in *Vogue* than in most scholarly books published in North America!) To counter *Vogue* (both British and American versions) I've written through issues of *Self* (a health/fitness magazine also geared to female readership) and *Prevention* (another "health" magazine). The non-magazine poems are included as a variant measure of linguistic origin, and an alternative to "mined" creativity.

Vanity Release (2003)

a statement re: "sourced" poems

I have become increasingly intrigued by late 19th and early 20th century shorthand dictionaries and manuals (and most recently a mid-20th-century typewriting manual), in addition to phrase books for travellers through the 20th century.

The choice of word lists, sentences to learn by, and the exercises in these respective manuals reflect not only the ongoing changes in North American English for this period, but also the shifts in educational, business, and technological terminology. To engage with these terms in a context of contemporary investigational poetic practice is one way to meaningfully perplex what is so easily taken for granted technologically, linguistically, and socially in our own times.

ACKNOWLEDGEMENTS

Thanks to all the editors and publishers responsible for publishing my poetry over the years.

Some of the poems first appeared in *Anerca*, *Antígona Editores Refractários*, *Cabaret Vert*, *Capilano Review*, *Contemporary Verse II*, *Dandelion*, *Filling Station*, *Hole*, *Open Letter*, *Poetry Canada Review*, *Precipice*, *Prism International*, *Queen Street Quarterly*, *Raddle Moon*, *Rampike*, *The Gig*, *Tessera*, *Westcoast Line*, *What!*, *Writing*, *Essex*, *Prague Literary Review*, *SALT*, *Sources*, *AND*, *Archeus*, *Fragmente*, *ON WORD*, *The Paper*, *Veer Off*, *Verse*, *1913 A Journal of Forms*, *AVEC*, *Big Allis*, *Damn the Caesars*, *Notus*, *Pilot*, *Primary Writing*, *Screens & Tasted Parallels*, *Sulfur*, *The Iowa Review*, *Triage* and online in *The East Village Poetry Web*, *lyric mailer*, *Riding the Meridian*, *phillytalk 19* (with Allen Fisher), *The Alterran Poetry Ensemble*, *GutCult* and *How2*.

My poetry titles have been published by Underwhich Editions, Nightwood Editions, Chax Press, West House Books, Bookthug, ECW Press, Coach House Books, House Press, Wild Honey Press and Zasterle Press.

Publishers of anthologies in which my work appears include Antigona, Coach House Books, LIT Verlag, Norsk Forfattersentrum, Samizdat Editions, Edições Afrontamento, POG and Chax Press, Talisman House, Insomniac Press, Reality Street Editions, Sun & Moon Press, Insomniac Press, Potes & Poets Press, and Nightwood Editions.

Special thanks to Jay Millar and Alan Halsey, and ongoingly to Steve McCaffery, whose poetic insights and "incites" are as provocative and challenging as ever.

Gratitude must also be expressed for funding received previously from the Canada Council for the Arts, Ontario Arts Council, and Toronto Arts Council.

BIBLIOGRAPHY

Excerpts from the following works by Karen Mac Cormack included in *Tale Light*:

Nothing by Mouth, Toronto: Underwhich Editions, 1984, (reprint) Toronto:
   Book Thug, 2003.
Straw Cupid, Toronto: Nightwood Editions, Toronto, 1987.
Quill Driver, London: Nightwood Editions, 1989.
PALM (broadside), Buffalo: Buffalo Broadsides No. 9, 1991.
Quirks & Quillets, Tucson: Chax Press, 1991.
Marine Snow, Toronto: ECW Press, Toronto, 1995.
The Tongue Moves Talk, Tucson: Chax Press/ Hay-on-Wye: West House Books,
   1997.
Multiplex (with Ron Silliman), Bray: Wild Honey Press, 1998.
At Issue, Toronto: Coach House Books, 2001.
Vanity Release, La Laguna, Tenerife: Zasterle Press, 2003.
Plural Modifiers (broadside), Sheffield: Gargoyle Editions, 2006.

Other titles by Karen Mac Cormack:

Fit to Print (with Alan Halsey), Toronto: Coach House Books/ Sheffield: West
   House Books, 1998.
From Implexures, Calgary: House Press, 2001.
From A Middle (with Steve McCaffery), Calgary: House Press, 2002 (reprint
   2003).
Implexures (*Volume 1*), Tucson: Chax Press/ Sheffield: West House Books, 2003.
Implexures (*Complete Edition*), Tucson: Chax Press/ Sheffield: West House Books,
   2008.

A NOTE ON THE TYPE

Joanna is a transitional serif typeface designed by Eric Gill (1882–1940) in the period 1930–31, and named for one of his daughters. The typeface was originally designed for proprietary use by Gill's printing shop Hague & Gill. The type was first produced in a small quantity by the Caslon Foundry for hand composition. It was eventually licensed for public release by the Monotype foundry in 1937.

In designing Joanna, Gill took inspiration from the types of Robert Granjon (1513–1589). The underlying armature of both the roman and italics bear strong similarities with Grandjon's type, yet the spare, sharp squared serifs and moderate contrast of strokes, have a twentieth century modernist feeling. The italics are more vertical than Grandjon's with only a 3° slope. The face is, as Gill described it himself "a book face free from all fancy business." Similarities can be seen with Gill's earlier typefaces Cockerel and Perpetua. Gill chose Joanna for setting *An Essay on Typography*, a book by Gill on his thoughts on typography, typesetting, and page design.[†]

Gill Sans was designed by Eric Gill and issued by Monotype in 1927. Gill Sans is a distinctly British but highly readable sans-serif, composed of latently humanist and overtly geometric forms. Text figures and small caps – very useful when the face is used for text work – were added by Monotype design staff in 1997.[††]

[†] Excerpted from Wikipedia.
[††] Excerpted from Robert Bringhurst's *The Elements of Typographic Style*, Hartley & Marks, 2002.

COLOPHON

Manufactured in an edition of 500 copies Spring 2010 by BookThug and West House Books. Distributed in Canada by the Literary Press Group and in the United Kingdom by West House Books. Both presses are distributed in America by Small Press Distribution. Shop online at www.westhousebooks.co.uk and www.bookthug.com.

BOOK
PRODUCTION
WAR ECONOMY
STANDARD